FANTASTICALLY GREAT WOMEN

SPORTS STARS

and their

STORIES

Books by
Kate Pankhurst

Fantastically Great Women
Who Changed the World

Fantastically Great Women
Who Made History

Fantastically Great Women
Who Worked Wonders

Fantastically Great Women
Who Saved the Planet

Fantastically Great Women
Scientists and Their Stories

Fantastically Great Women
Artists and Their Stories

We Are All Astronauts!

We Are All Inventors!

Praise for *Fantastically Great Women Scientists and their Stories*

Shortlisted for the Sainsbury's Children's Book Awards 2021 in the Learning and Development category

"It deploys just the right amount of lovely, fascinating detail to inform and inspire." – *The Guardian*

Praise for *Fantastically Great Women Artists and their Stories*

"Anyone with a love of art will enjoy this book from the fun FANTASTICALLY GREAT WOMEN series." – *The Week Junior*

"Discover some amazingly talented women artists in this handy non-fiction guide … it's full of fascinating facts and stories to inspire the artist in anyone." – *WRD Magazine*

Praise for the Fantastically Great Women books

"With their playful use of speech bubbles and perspective shifts, Pankhurst's books remain significantly more engaging and inspiring than the rival *Rebel Girls*." – Imogen Russell Williams, *The Guardian*

"It's a tremendously engaging read: smart, informative, inclusive and accessible, with gorgeous, visually creative art. The tone is really joyful and it's hard to imagine any group of primary-aged children who wouldn't be inspired by these stories."
– Fiona Noble, *The Bookseller*

"So many worthy nonfiction books for this age group have good intentions but fail to step beyond simple preaching with boring line drawings. This one succeeds, thanks to its interesting choice of role models, gorgeous colourful illustrations, a sense of humour and sharp language that informs without patronising."
– *The Times*

"An absolute must-have for every young person's bookshelf."
– *The Huffington Post*

"It's impossible not to be inspired by this book."
– *Absolutely Education*

"This book which is a must have for anybody – girl or boy, man or woman – it's enlightening for one and all ... it's celebratory."
– *Books for Keeps*

"Every element of this book is pieced together perfectly."
– *Acorn Books*

Kate Pankhurst

FANTASTICALLY GREAT WOMEN SPORTS STARS and their STORIES

BLOOMSBURY
CHILDREN'S BOOKS
LONDON   OXFORD   NEW YORK   NEW DELHI   SYDNEY

First published 2024 by Bloomsbury Publishing Plc
BLOOMSBURY CHILDREN'S BOOKS
Bloomsbury Publishing Plc
50 Bedford Square, London WC1B 3DP, UK
29 Earlsfort Terrace, Dublin 2, Ireland

BLOOMSBURY, BLOOMSBURY CHILDREN'S BOOKS and the Diana logo
are trademarks of Bloomsbury Publishing Plc

First published in Great Britain in 2024 by Bloomsbury Publishing Plc

ISBN: PB: 978 15266 1548 0
eBook: 978 15266 9610 0

10 9 8 7 6 5 4 3 2 1

Printed and bound by CPI Group (UK) Ltd, Croydon CR0 4YY

MIX
Paper | Supporting
responsible forestry
FSC® C171272
FSC
www.fsc.org

To find out more about our authors and books visit www.bloomsbury.com and
sign up for our newsletters

For the girls and boys at
Calverley United Junior Football Club,
you are fantastically great sports stars
of grassroots football.

Contents

WOMEN in Sport

The story of women in top-level sport was, for a very long time, the story of being told 'no'.

No, women aren't allowed to play.

No, women ought not to do things like that.

No, women can't compete with men.

And no, women's sports *don't* count.

NO!

The eight fantastically great women sports stars in this book have one thing in common: they didn't take NO for an answer.

The ancient Olympic Games were set up only for men. **Cynisca**, the Spartan princess, fought back when she used a loophole in the rules to become the first woman ever to win a laurel wreath at the Games.

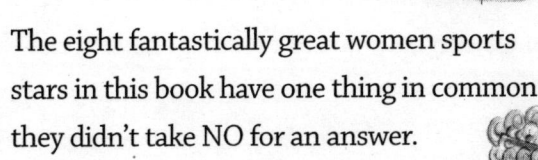

1

The all-rounder **Lottie Dod** became the first megastar sportswoman. She was a tennis and golf champion, played hockey for England, was the first woman to toboggan down the Cresta Run and even won an Olympic medal in archery!

Very few other Olympic sports were open to women – until amazing organiser **Alice Milliat** stepped in. She set up her own rival games and forced the Olympics to let more women in. And the achievements of those women have been incredible ever since.

But not everyone wants to compete, of course. Sometimes sport is about doing the thing you love for its own sake. And women have just as much right as anyone else to take up sports just for the thrill of it. Japanese mountaineer **Junko Tabei** was the first woman ever to reach the summit (top) of Mount Everest – but she did it because she loved the climbing, not the applause afterwards.

Yet some people were born for the competition! **Derartu Tulu**, a long-distance runner, comes from a small town in Ethiopia with only basic training facilities. But that town produces some of the world's greatest runners! Derartu was the first Black African woman to win an Olympic gold medal. But many more have followed in her fast footsteps.

Marta Vieira da Silva, the greatest woman footballer of all time, played in five Olympics, twice took Brazil to Olympic finals and was the first ever footballer to score in five World Cups. And she achieved all this when, not many years before, women's football had been actually illegal in her home country!

Fantastically great women sports stars have overcome all kinds of obstacles to achieve their goals. Sportswomen with disabilities hear 'no' even more often than everyone else. The amazing **Paralympic** victories of swimmer **Ellie Simmonds** are a marvellous example of what talent, hard work and determination can do.

The incredible gymnast **Simone Biles** had to overcome a hard childhood and has faced up to many problems. Now she is widely recognised as the greatest gymnast of all time, with a spectacular haul of Olympic golds.

These are just a few of the fantastically great women sports stars, past and present, who have trained hard, used their talent and never taken 'no' for an answer. They've reached the top, and shown everyone what women can do.

Prepare to be inspired!

CYNISCA

BORN AROUND 440 BCE
THE FIRST WOMAN TO CHASE OLYMPIC GLORY AND CATCH IT!

Cynisca was a princess. She was an athlete. She was a proud **Spartan**. And, most importantly, she was great at spotting **loopholes** ...

The **modern Olympic Games** are a global event in which the best sportsmen and sportswomen from across the whole world come together to compete against each other.

Baron Pierre de Coubertin started the modern Olympic games in Athens, 1896. I made sure that women got a place in them! Find out more on page 51.

OLYMPICS 1896

When the **Ancient Games** first began, many years ago, the Olympics were only for men. Until Cynisca changed things.

Who is SHE?

EH?

WHAT?

It's all about ME!

The ancient Olympic Games began **3,000 years ago** as a religious ceremony. They were held in Olympia, a big **sacred** site in southern Greece with a large number of temples dedicated to the many **Greek gods**. The king of the gods was called Zeus, and the Olympics were held in his honour. Originally, the Olympic Games were only for Greek people. In those days, Greece wasn't a single country, but was made up of a lot of independent city-states, including **Athens** and **Sparta**.

They often fought one another. But every four years, the fighting stopped for the Olympics! The cities would all agree a **truce**, meaning that the athletes and spectators could travel safely to Olympia. Everyone came together from the **rival cities** to enjoy the Olympics and cheer for their athletes. Then they went home ... and the wars would start all over again!

BOO!

· WELCOME TO OLYMPIA ·

Olympia was made up of a religious area called the Altis (which was marked by a boundary wall), and a secular (non-religious) area located outside the wall.

· THE ALTIS ·

The Altis contained the sacred temples and was where offerings were kept and sacrifices were made.

The secular area was where the training areas and competition sites stood, plus other buildings used for the administration of the Olympics, or to welcome important guests.

GYMNASIUM

HIPPODROME

Only the priests and staff lived at Olympia all the time, so it was usually very quiet ... until, once every four years, it came alive with athletes, spectators and merchants who sold food and souvenirs to the crowds. It's thought more than 40,000 people might have come to each Olympic Games.

It was a strict rule that all the athletes had to be male, Greek and **freeborn** – meaning they could not be slaves. Slavery was common in ancient Greece, and slaves weren't allowed to be involved in politics or public life. Women couldn't compete either – and most of them weren't even allowed to watch! Only young **unmarried** girls and one priestess could be spectators at the Olympics. Married women were completely banned from being spectators. If they tried to sneak in and were caught, the punishment was **death**. This would sometimes involve hurling the rule-breakers off the side of the mountain!

COME AND RUN AT THE
HERAEA GAMES

Some historical records suggest that the ancient Greeks held a separate festival called the **Heraea Games** where girls could compete in running races to honour Zeus's wife, the goddess Hera.

Unfortunately, there is not much evidence left to tell us about it. What we know about ancient history is limited by what was written down. But in those days most people, especially women, couldn't read or write, and very little of what did get written has survived the past 3,000 years!

We are the WINNERS!

It isn't **surprising** that women weren't allowed to watch the Olympics. Most ancient Greek women didn't have a lot of **freedom**. Men believed they were superior to women, so it was the men who were in charge and who made the laws – while women were expected to have babies and look after the **home** and **children**. Most ancient Greek women weren't even supposed to go out and exercise, let alone play games and compete with other people.

Shhh ... DON'T tell anyone!

But one Greek city-state was different. In Sparta, women were expected to be fit and athletic with well-trained bodies. The Spartans were very **warlike** people, and believed that strong healthy women would have strong children, who would make good **soldiers**. Spartan women had a lot more freedom and education than other women of the time.

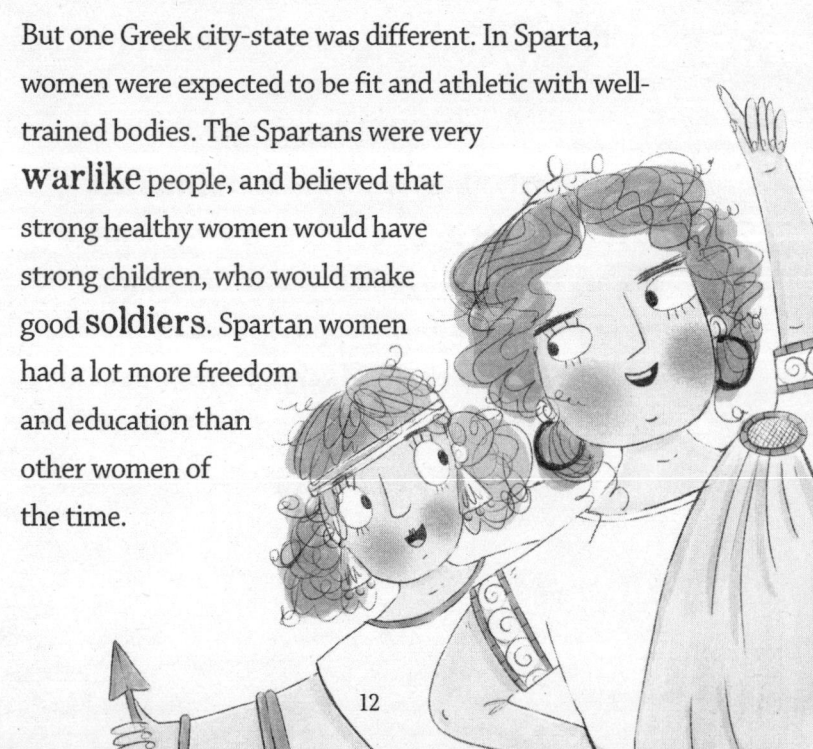

Cynisca was a Spartan **princess** born around 440 BCE. She was the daughter of King Archidamus II of Sparta. Her name means 'little female dog' – we might call her 'Puppy Girl'. (She was probably named after her **famous** grandfather, who had the nickname *Cyniscus*, or 'small dog'.)

Being a princess, Cynisca didn't have to work. But, like all Spartan women, she trained hard. She would have done all kinds of sports, such as running, jumping, **javelin** and **discus throw**, and would also have learned dance and poetry. And, as a princess, she might even have been taught how to read and write. Certainly she would have been given a lot more **education** than most other Greek women.

Spartan women learned to work with **horses**. They might ride, drive horse-drawn vehicles and race one another in two-horse chariots. But Cynisca wanted more than that. Ever since she was a little girl, she dreamed about **racing** her horses not just against other women, but at the Olympic Games themselves.

Chariot racing was an important Olympic event. Teams of two or four horses were driven round and round a racecourse called a **hippodrome**.

No one knows for sure how the Olympic Games started. Olympia is in the Peloponnese area of Greece, named after the hero Pelops. According to the poems of the Greek poet Pindar, Pelops asked the god Poseidon for a fast chariot in order to win an important chariot race. One popular **myth** suggests that Pelops's victory was the inspiration for the first Olympic Games. If so, then chariot racing was perhaps the first Olympic sport!

I'll send you a fast chariot!

Thanks!

The Olympic Games were held to **honour** Zeus, but they were also a great way for rich men to show off how **wealthy** and **powerful** they were! Chariot racing was a very expensive sport, as good horses and chariots cost a lot of money. It wasn't a sport for ordinary people.

It was also very **dangerous**. The chariots could overturn easily, especially when going around the bends or when the horses crashed into one another. The drivers were sometimes killed or badly hurt because of this, so the rich owners who bought and trained the horses mostly used **professional** drivers, often slaves – they didn't want to risk their own lives! A few owners drove the chariots themselves, if they were particularly brave and skilful, but most people thought that was **showing off**!

It's MY chariot, so I win!

You might be thinking, 'But slaves couldn't take part in the Olympics!' And you're right, they couldn't – but in chariot racing, the rule was that the drivers didn't count. Even though they were the ones doing all the work and risking their lives! Most records of the time don't even name the drivers. It was the owner who mattered – and the *owner* of the winning team would be awarded the victory wreath.

That's where Cynisca saw her chance.

· OLYMPIC RULES ·

- ALL ATHLETES MUST BE MEN
- NO WOMEN IN THE ARENA
- THE CHARIOT OWNER DOESN'T HAVE TO DRIVE THE CHARIOT
- THE CHARIOT OWNER WINS THE VICTORY WREATH
- THE CHARIOT OWNER DOESN'T HAVE TO ATTEND THE RACE

Cynisca had found a **loophole** in the rules. There was nothing to say that the owner of a chariot team had to be a man. That meant a woman *could* compete in the Olympic Games – as long as she could afford to run her own horses. Cynisca saw her way in!

Luckily, Cynisca was **rich**. Her father, the king, had left her enough money to be able to pay for her own horses and chariots. And her brother, who became King Agesilaus II, supported her, even though no woman had **ever** competed at the Olympic Games before.

The historian Xenophon says that Agesilaus wanted Cynisca to win because it would prove that chariot racing was only about the owner's wealth, not about skill and bravery. But Xenophon was Athenian, and Athenian men didn't approve of women doing anything!

XENOPHON

Ignore him.

Many modern historians believe that Agesilaus wanted her to win because having an Olympic champion in the family would make them look good. Athens had won a string of famous victories in Olympic horse racing, so maybe Agesilaus wanted to prove that a Spartan woman was better than Athenian men.

Or maybe he was just a good brother who wanted his sister to win because it would make her happy!

Hey Sis, make sure you WIN! I'll look GOOD.

Cynisca chose the Olympic event called *tethrippon*, or four-horse chariot racing. This was a hard, dangerous sport. The horses had to be perfectly trained to keep calm in the **exciting** atmosphere. They had to all work together to race as **fast** as they could around ten or twelve laps of the hippodrome, without crashing into any other teams. The turns at each end were especially dangerous, and this is where drivers were often hurt or killed when chariots overturned.

Cynisca entered her first team at the Olympic Games of 396 BCE, when she was in her forties, using male charioteers to drive the horses she had trained. And guess what? She **won**! And then, in the next Olympic Games she did it **again**. She had won **two** Olympic victory wreaths.

YAY!

Most historians agree she wasn't allowed to drive the horses in the race herself. But the wreath always went to the owner, and so she was the winner fair and square. Runners and fast ships brought the news back home to Sparta, and all over Greece:

Princess Puppy Girl has WON for SPARTA! A woman is an OLYMPIC CHAMPION!

Cynisca wanted to make sure everyone knew about her victory. She paid for a set of **bronze statues** of herself and her winning team – horses, chariot and driver – to be built at the entranceway of the Temple of Zeus in Olympia. Nobody could go in without seeing the woman who'd won the races! And she had the statues inscribed (written on) so nobody would miss the point:

"Kings of Sparta were my fathers and brothers. I, Cynisca, victorious at the chariot race with her swift-footed horses, erected this statue. I claim that I am the only woman in all Greece who has won this crown."

Cynisca's fame spread across Greece. The Spartans were **delighted** with her victory. She was given a hero-shrine in a sacred place called the Plane Tree Grove and **worshipped** as a hero after her death.

Several other Greek women went on to become famous in chariot racing, **inspired** by Cynisca, the first woman to win an Olympic victory. Even if she couldn't compete herself, she showed that women **belonged** in the sporting arena.

Cynisca was the **first** sporting heroine. And she wouldn't be the **last**. But it would take a long time, and many more determined women, to change things for everyone.

CHARLOTTE 'LOTTIE' DOD

THE GIRL WHO COULD DO IT ALL!

When you think about the **Victorian period,** you might imagine women in **huge dresses,** sitting at home and not showing their ankles. People don't often remember it as a great time for women's sport! But Lottie Dod proves that wrong. She is one of the most **talented** female athletes of all time, and some of her records still stand today.

Gosh!

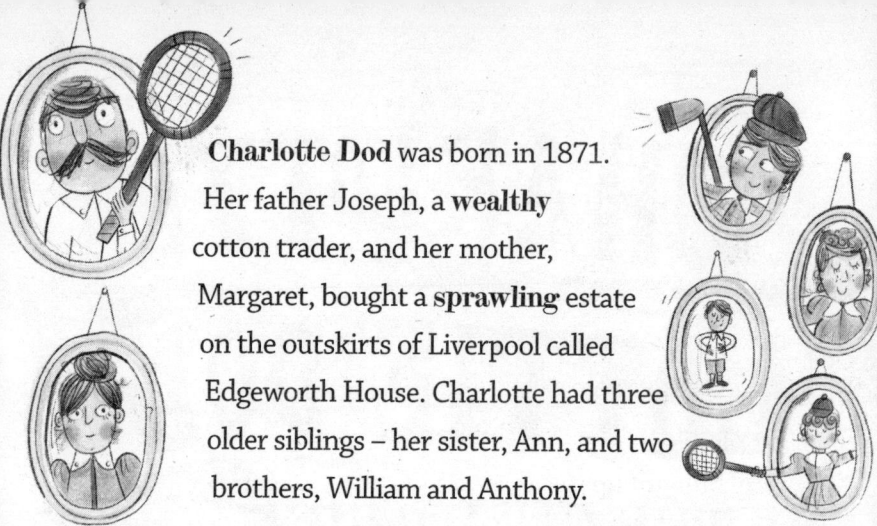

Charlotte Dod was born in 1871. Her father Joseph, a **wealthy** cotton trader, and her mother, Margaret, bought a **sprawling** estate on the outskirts of Liverpool called Edgeworth House. Charlotte had three older siblings – her sister, Ann, and two brothers, William and Anthony.

The Sporting News

Crowds cheer her name!

Her family called her 'Lottie', and – when she later became famous – so did the newspapers and the crowds when they cheered her name. She hated it. "Pray do not call me Lottie," she once told a reporter, "My name is Charlotte and I hate to be called Lottie in public."

Nevertheless, she was always called Lottie.

During this period, wealthy Victorians – women as well as men – were very interested in health and sport.

Weightlifting, bodybuilding, rowing machines and modern-looking gymnasiums were all becoming very popular. The Dod children were brought up to run, swim, shoot and play many different kinds of ball games.

All the Dods were **sporty**. Ann was excellent at tennis and billiards (a game similar to pool or snooker). William would become an Olympic gold-winning **archer**.

Anthony was a mountain climber and chess champion.

And Lottie was …

Something SPECIAL.

The first sport that Lottie really got into was **lawn tennis** (which we now just call tennis). This sport had only been invented around the 1870s but it quickly became hugely **popular**. Joseph had courts set up in Edgeworth House's grounds so the Dod children could play regularly. Lottie proved to be an extremely **gifted** player. She played in her first **tournament** aged eleven, partnered in doubles with her sister Ann, who was almost nine years older than her. Lottie won her first singles title in 1885, at a tournament in

Go, Lottie!

Waterloo. But her real rise to stardom came when she almost beat Wimbledon ladies' **champion** Maud Watson in the final of the 1885 Northern Championships in Manchester, UK. The following year, at the West of England Championships, Lottie defeated Watson to claim a decisive singles title. She was still only 14. The press started calling her 'Little Wonder'.

WIMBLEDON
All England Croquet and Lawn Tennis Club

The All England Croquet and Lawn Tennis Club, based in Wimbledon, south London, UK, held its first Lawn Tennis Championships in 1877, in which the only event was Gentlemen's Singles. The club added the Ladies' Singles in 1884. Ladies' Doubles and Mixed Doubles didn't come until 1913. The annual Wimbledon Championships is now widely considered the world's most important tennis tournament in the world.

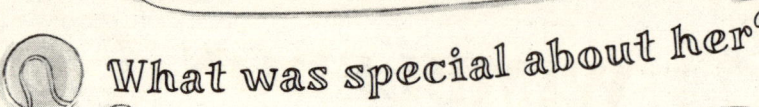

What was special about her?

Lottie was fierce and fast, and played with a lot of power. In those days, tennis was often played in a gentler way, with long rallies (players hitting the ball back and forth). Lottie had no time for that! She told women that they could win if they:

"Go in for it heartily, and do not merely frivol at garden parties."

fig A:
Forehand

She was also one of the first players to use different grips for forehand and backhand shots. Rackets were heavy wooden objects then, and you needed to be skilful to shift grip quickly.

fig B:
Backhand

Another thing Lottie had on her side was that she could dress more sensibly than other female players. Victorian women tennis players didn't wear the short skirts or shorts that players wear today, but long formal skirts that came down to their feet. Because Lottie was so young, she was allowed to wear shorter dresses, ones that came to a few inches above her ankles. This gave her a bit more mobility.

fig C:
Tennis attire

And she had the right attitude:

fig D:
Determined

"I never lose my head in a game, and experience has taught me never to lose my temper. Tennis is a capital game to teach a girl self-control."

In 1887, Lottie entered the Wimbledon Ladies' Singles
Championship. She was a **star** from the very first match.
Tall and steely-eyed, she played **ferociously**, smashing
shots past her opponents. The crowd loved it and chanted
her name as she beat the **defending champion** Blanche
Bingley in straight sets.

Lottie was fifteen. She is still the **youngest ever**
Wimbledon Ladies' Singles Champion.

Lottie won Wimbledon again in 1888. That year, aged
sixteen, she invited three male tennis champions to play
her in **exhibition matches** (where they weren't competing
for a prize). This was an **astonishing**
thing for a Victorian woman to do.
Everyone still believed that men were
better than women at all sports, so
for Lottie to challenge **three**
of the top male players showed
amazing confidence.

It wasn't a bitter battle, though. Lottie knew all the men well, and had partnered two of them in mixed doubles. They all insisted on giving her a two-point **advantage** to make up for her hampering **long skirts**. (One of them had once dressed in women's clothes to play against Blanche Bingley as a dare, so he knew how difficult it was!)

WHACK!

Ooomph!

The first match was against Wimbledon doubles winner Ernest Renshaw – Lottie won the first set but lost the match, though it was **hard fought**. In the second match, she **thrashed** Scottish champion Harry Grove. Finally, in the third, she wiped the floor with six-time Wimbledon champion William Renshaw (Ernest's twin). She had **beaten** two of the best male players of her time.

Lottie was expected to defend her Wimbledon title in 1889 – but instead she took the next year off tennis. The official reason was because she was on a sailing holiday. But there were other things going on ...

Joseph Dod had died when Lottie was eight, and since then Margaret, her mother, became very **controlling**. She insisted the girls should be home-schooled, which was normal for the time, but she wouldn't let the boys go to school or university **either**. And when they became adults, she didn't want them to get jobs or **marry**.

Then in 1889, Ann fell in love and asked her mother for her blessing to get married. But Margaret **refused**! Ann had to decide whether to follow her heart, or obey her mother – and she chose to run away and get married. She wrote letters to Margaret every day, but Margaret returned them all **unopened**. Ann's children believed that Margaret refused to let Lottie go to Wimbledon in 1889 because she wanted to keep her remaining daughter at home.

Lottie finally returned to the tennis circuit full time in 1891. It had been a while since she played **competitively**, but she wasn't at all rusty. She won all but one of the many matches she played for the next few years. She even won Wimbledon three years in a row – a feat that wouldn't be equalled for another thirty years! She was now the most famous sportswoman in the world.

Lottie was **outspoken** when it came to women's tennis. She argued against men who said women couldn't play or understand sport, and also called for sensible, **practical** sports clothing for women. She even offered excellent advice to other women on **training** and **technique**.

After ten years of playing competitive tennis, Lottie was about as close to **unbeatable** as it was possible to be. And, for her, that meant tennis just wasn't a challenge anymore!

She had no interest in staying at the top for the sake of it. She liked the **competition**. And if she didn't have anyone to compete with in tennis, she'd need to find something else!

Hmmm ... what's next?

Lottie's father had left his children very well off. They didn't need to work, and their mother Margaret would not allow them to get jobs even if they wanted to. Without tennis to occupy her, Lottie had time on her hands and money to spend. She wanted to see the **world**, and she wanted new challenges. She found those in **winter sports**.

In 1895, Lottie and her brother Anthony first went to St Moritz, an Alpine resort in Switzerland famous for figure skating. Lottie trained for more than two hours a day for two months in order to pass the **famously difficult** St Moritz Ladies' Skating Test. And she did it! The next year, she took the far harder Men's Test and became the second ever woman to pass it.

But Lottie was always on the lookout for a new challenge …

After taking up tobogganing, she set her sights on tackling the **Cresta Run**. This was a fast, sometimes deadly, ¾-mile roller coaster of a track, on which tobogganers could reach speeds of 70 miles per hour (mph).

THE CRESTA RUN

At this time, the world's fastest cars could travel at only around 15 mph. A racehorse might get up to speeds of about 50 mph, but only for a few minutes. To go any faster, you would have to be a passenger in one of a handful of express trains in the USA. The Cresta Run was like nothing else on Earth.

It was thought to be far too dangerous for women, and only a few had tackled parts of it. But that didn't put Lottie off. She asked her friend Harold Topham, a **gold medallist** on the Cresta Run, to coach her. In the season from 1896 to 1897, she became the first woman **ever** to do the whole Cresta Run!

For a while, Lottie's life revolved around winter sports and European travel. She took up curling (where you slide stones along the ice towards a goal), ice hockey, bobsledding (sliding down ice in a sled, called a 'bob') and ice cricket. Then she and Anthony went on a bicycling tour through Italy, Switzerland, San Marino and France. For an additional **challenge**, Lottie began mountaineering with her friend, the mountaineer Elizabeth Main, and together they climbed some of Europe's most difficult peaks.

Eventually, Lottie fell out with Elizabeth. Her travels were over, and she and Anthony settled back home in Edgeworth.

Being home meant she needed a new **challenge** to conquer. So, not one to sit around, she took up yet another new sport – field hockey. Unusually for a women's game, it was a **violent** sport which led to a lot of bruises and **injuries**. But, of course, Lottie was great at it! Soon enough, she became captain of the Cheshire county team and played forward for the English **national** team in 1899 and 1900, scoring both **goals** to win the 1900 England-Ireland match.

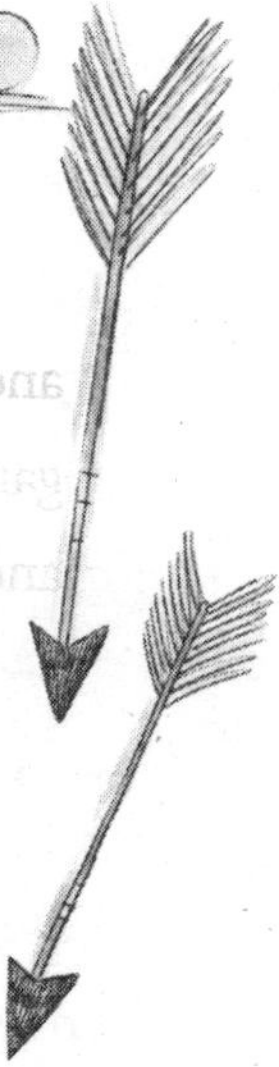

As she had with tennis, Lottie lost interest in hockey once she'd reached the top. Instead, she took up horse-riding and rowing, practised archery and became one of the best billiards players in England (though her sister Ann was even better).

Meanwhile, she was also playing golf. She had found golf a difficult sport to master, which in Lottie terms meant that she was a regular competitor in the National Championships, but – unusually for her – she had only reached the semi-finals **twice** by 1900.

Then everything changed …

The Dod family's sporting life came to an abrupt halt when their mother died in 1901. With Margaret gone, the three unmarried Dod children could **finally** leave home. Lottie and her brothers sold Edgeworth House and moved to Newbury in Berkshire to be near Ann and her children. Anthony got married and had his own family. Lottie and William never did.

Lottie and her siblings barely played any sports for a couple of years. It wouldn't have seemed right to play while in mourning (grieving), and they had to get used to life without their mother. Lottie eventually returned to golf to compete in the 1904 British Ladies' Amateur tournament in Scotland. She won, making her the **first** and **only** woman to win British tennis and golf championships. It made headlines around the world.

Lottie was now an **international** star, and she travelled to the USA to compete as a golfer. Unfortunately, for once in Lottie's life, she wasn't on form. She was suffering from sciatica (nerve pain) and fatigue, and lost most of her matches.

SPORTS TODAY

WHAT HAS HAPPENED TO LOTTIE?

It was a very unusual experience for her. When she returned to Britain she also struggled to recapture her previous winning streak. It was very difficult for her to accept.

This is VERY hard for me – I'm not used to losing!

Not one to let anything stop her, Lottie decided it was time to try **something else**. In 1906, she joined an archery club and, back on true Lottie form, won a major competition – just a few months after she began serious training. In 1908, she was selected for the **Olympics**.

The Olympic Games did not welcome women. Pierre de Coubertin, the president of the International Olympic Committee, thought that the competition ought to be an "exaltation of male athleticism", in which women's only role was to applaud the men. He said women's sports were "against the laws of nature".

I'll show you!

Women in sport? What piffle!

There were more than 2,000 competitors at the 1908 Olympics – but only 37 of them were women! The archery event included 25 of the women, and Lottie faced fellow Briton Sybil 'Queenie' Newall in the final. It was a close match in which Lottie was narrowly beaten. She came home with **silver**. Her brother William won **gold**.

When she was 38, Lottie narrowly missed winning the archery Grand National – had she been successful, she would have been a British champion in three different sports. Sadly, she came second. Her sciatica was getting worse and worse. It put an end to a sporting career that had lasted almost 30 years.

During the **First World War**, Lottie served as a nurse in British hospitals because the sciatica made her unable to travel to France. She received a **Red Cross Service Medal** for her hard work. In later life, looking for something new to do, she turned to music – and, of course, was marvellous at it. She had an **excellent** voice, joined many choirs and regularly performed in concerts. Whatever Lottie did, she strived for **greatness**. She always wanted to live up to her own motto:

In Lottie's lifetime, women's sport became increasingly professional, but she wasn't sure she liked it. It seemed to her that in order to get to the top, players had to devote so much **time** to their game that they lost half the **enjoyment**.

Lottie never missed Wimbledon until she was too old to make the trip to the All England Club. She died in 1960, aged 88, listening to Wimbledon on the **radio**.

The *Guinness Book of Records* named her the most **versatile** female athlete of all time. One of the Wimbledon chiefs wrote of her, "So versatile was she, so talented at whatever sport she tried her hand at, that it is a pity that flying had not then been invented; I feel sure Miss Lottie Dod would have been the first girl to make a solo flight around the world."

And I would have loved it!

Lottie Dod, the Little Wonder, changed people's ideas about women in sport. She proved that women could play as hard as men, and that the world was ready for women athletes. Now they just needed the chance to show it …

Born in 1884 in Nantes, France, **Alice Milliat** was the eldest of five children. At the age of twenty, she went to England, where she met and married a Frenchman named Joseph Milliat who, by coincidence, was also from Nantes. Alice was **sporty**. She took up rowing as a hobby while she lived in England, as well as swimming and playing hockey.

But, very sadly, after only four years of marriage Joseph died. He and Alice had no children, so she was left alone. To deal with her grief, Alice went **travelling** around Europe on her own. She learned languages easily, and when she returned to France at the start of the First World War, she took a job as a **translator**.

But Alice's real love was sport, and particularly **sports administration**.

Alice became **president** of a women's sports club called Fémina Sport in 1915. She organised events and **planned** what the club should do. A couple of years later, three women's clubs (including Fémina Sport) joined forces and set up a brand new organisation called the Fédération des Sociétés Féminines Sportives de France (**Federation** of Women's Sports Clubs – FSFSF). Its aim was to promote supposedly '**unfeminine**' sports, such as athletics, running, swimming, rowing, field hockey and football.

GO, GIRLS!

Most of the FSFSF founders were men, including the first president. But Alice knew that if the FSFSF was going to help women, it needed to have a woman in charge. Alice took over as president in 1919, and from then on it was run by **women**. With her brilliant organisational skills, the FSFSF grew and grew, and by 1925, it included

four hundred clubs – having started off with just three!

The FSFSF set up the first organised **French women's football championship** in 1919. Alice's club Fémina Sport won the first championship, although there were only two teams playing, so the competition wasn't that fierce!

As the leader of the FSFSF, Alice looked for ways to get more attention for women's football. In 1920, the **league** sent a team to play in England, where women's football was **extremely** popular. The international matches attracted **big** crowds, and the return match played in Paris was watched by 22,000 supporters. The league grew to 16 teams by 1924. Women's football was on the **rise**, and Alice wrote articles promoting the game in various French magazines.

But many men argued that playing football was **bad** for women's health, and not a **proper** way to behave. The English Football Association (FA) **banned** women's football from their grounds in 1921. They said:

THE RULES: NO GIRLS

"Football is quite unsuitable for females and should not be encouraged."

Many other European countries followed suit, and in 1933 women's football was banned by the French Football Federation (FFF). The ban would not be lifted until 1974, over **50 years later**.

The English Football Association
NO GIRLS ALLOWED

The FA didn't re-admit women's teams for 50 years, and women's football was actually against the law in Brazil until 1979. Men **really did** have a problem with women playing football! Maybe that's because it had got too popular for their liking: a women's match played at Liverpool's Goodison Park in 1920 attracted 53,000 spectators. The FA ban came into force shortly afterwards. Alice Norris, one of the most famous English footballers of the 1920s, said the Football Association was just jealous because the women were getting bigger crowds.

This isn't fair!

They are JUST jealous.

The modern Olympic Games

The Olympic Games were originally a sacred festival for Greeks, but went into decline after the Romans conquered Greece. The last recorded ancient Olympic Games were held in 393 CE.

In the 1880s, an **aristocratic** French historian named Pierre de Coubertin had the idea to revive the Olympics as a modern athletics competition. He founded the International Olympics Committee (IOC) in 1894, and the first modern Olympics was held in Athens in 1896. Unfortunately, just like the original Olympics, only **men** were **allowed** to compete.

Pierre de Coubertin

Coubertin thought the Olympics should celebrate men, and didn't believe that women should be involved **at all**!

Nobody wants to see women EXERT themselves!

Thankfully, he didn't entirely get his way. The Paris 1900 Olympics allowed women to participate in only five events: golf, croquet, sailing, tennis and horse riding. Later on, swimming, gymnastics, skating and archery were added to the women's repertoire. But the IOC flatly refused to let women compete in the highest profile **track and field** events.

PHEW!
I'm sweaty!

Track and field events are the ones that involve running, jumping and throwing. Some of these are races – from sprinting to marathons – but events also include long jump, high jump, pole vault, shot put and javelin. The IOC didn't like women doing any of these events because they might get sweaty!

Alice Milliat had **no time** for Coubertin's ideas.

Women's sport has its place in social life in the same way as men's!

As president of the FSFSF, Alice asked the International Association of Athletics Federations (IAAF) to include women's track and field in the 1924 Olympics. The answer was **no**. Men didn't want women athletes.

So the women did it **themselves**. Alice organised the first ever international women's multiple-sport event, known as the 1921 **Women's Olympiad**. It was held in Monte Carlo in March 1921, and 100 athletes from five nations took part – France, Great Britain, Italy, Norway and Switzerland. The athletes competed in ten events: running at various distances including 800 metres (m), hurdles, high jump, long jump, javelin and shot put. There were also exhibition events in basketball and gymnastics.

But Alice didn't attend the 1921 Olympiad. The chair of the 1921 Women's Olympiad organising committee was a man called Marcel Delabre, who was vice-president of the French Athletics Federation (FFA). This organisation was run by men, and it became clear that the FFA wanted to take **control** of women's athletics. Alice didn't like that at all, so she refused to support it.

Instead, she set up the Fédération Sportive Féminine Internationale (International Women's Sports Federation – FSFI), with Czechoslovakia (now the Czech Republic), France, Italy, Great Britain, Spain and the USA as the first countries to join. The FSFI asked to join the next Olympic Games, but the International Olympic Committee **refused**.

So, once again, Alice did it **herself**. In August 1922, the Jeux Olympiques Féminins (Women's Olympic Games) took place in Paris. It was a one-day event in which five countries competed in eleven events, and attracted a crowd of 20,000 spectators – and over a dozen **world records** were broken that day! Alice chose Paris as the venue because it was where Pierre de Coubertin lived, and she wanted to make him realise women's sport **mattered** too!

The IOC wasn't happy. They particularly didn't like the games being called 'Olympic'. So Alice made them a **deal**: she'd change the name if they added an extra **ten**

women's events to the official Olympic Games in 1928. Alice kept her side of the bargain. In 1926, the Women's Olympic Games became the Women's World Games, and ten countries participated. But the IOC broke their word. Only five women's track and field events were added to the 1928 Olympic programme instead of the ten they had promised. Alice was **furious**. The powerful British Women's Athletics Association **boycotted** the 1928 Olympics because of the way they'd been **lied** to.

The 800 m disaster

Although women were allowed to run in the 1928 Olympics, a lot of men still disapproved. They were particularly angry about the 800 m race, which they decided was too long and too demanding for women.

The *New York Times* reported: "The final of the women's 800-metre run, in which Lina Radke of Germany set a world's record, plainly demonstrated that even this distance makes too great a call on feminine strength. At the finish, six out of the nine runners were completely exhausted and fell headlong on the ground."

RUNNING SHOES FOR LADIES!

In reality, male athletes regularly fell down exhausted after the 800 m race, but according to the media when women did the same thing it showed they weren't strong enough.

Other journalists simply lied. Sports writer John Tunis described the final as, "Eleven wretched women, five of whom dropped out before the finish." In fact, nine runners started the race, and all of them finished.

But the media had decided what the story would be, and the IOC supported them. As a result, women wouldn't be allowed to race in the 800 m again until Rome 1960.

However, the women were not going to **give up**.
The next Women's World Games was held in 1930, in
Prague. Athletes from 17 nations competed in 12 track
and field events. Then in 1934, the Women's World Games
was held in London. It was the biggest yet, adding the
pentathlon and involving 19 countries. 15,000 spectators
came to watch.

With the success of Alice's Women's World Games,
Alice decided it was time to give the IOC and IAAF an
ultimatum. She told them that either there should be a full
programme of women's events at the 1936 Olympics – or
it should have **no women at all**. The Olympics should be
a men-only competition, and all women's sports should be
governed by the FSFI. She was tired of crumbs from the
men's table.

This caused a big **debate**. The IAAF argued that most athletes wanted men and women's sports to be managed by **one** organisation. Alice reminded them that she had only set up the FSFI because the IAAF had refused to support women's sports in the first place! She was willing to give up the FSFI and the Women's World Games if women could be fairly **represented** at international competitions.

It's a success!

Under Alice, the FSFI had become a worldwide success. The IAAF realised it had made a mistake, and decided to take back **control** of women's sport while they still could. They appointed a special commission (team of people) which agreed that the IAAF would take over international women's athletics. In return, there would be an expanded programme of nine events for women at the next Olympics, and they would recognise all the **world records** set in the Women's World Games.

It wasn't everything Alice had hoped for. But she'd got the IAAF to accept that women's athletics mattered, and to agree to **promote** them instead of trying to **stop** them. She'd proved that women's sport could be successful – so successful, in fact, that the big organisations didn't want to have to compete **against** them.

There was nothing more Alice could do. The FSFI never met again, and she gave up her involvement in sport. She died in 1957. She wasn't a well-known figure then, but her **impact** is recognised now. The Alice Milliat Foundation is a French organisation that promotes women's sport in her name, and in 2021, a statue of Alice was unveiled at the **headquarters** of the French Olympic Committee in Paris.

She is a LEGEND!

I didn't mess around!

During her lifetime, Alice was a controversial figure. She spoke her mind **bluntly**, and made **uncompromising** demands. She wasn't patient or persuasive when she thought people were **wrong**. That would have been quite normal in a man, but women were expected to be a lot nicer. Alice wasn't afraid of making enemies.

And she got things done. Against relentless opposition, Alice forced the male sports establishment to **accept** international women's sport. Without her, sports historians agree, it would have taken much longer for the IOC to accept women's full engagement in the Olympics.

SEOUL

TOKYO

It took a very long time for things to get better. As recently as the Seoul Games in 1988, women made up only about 25 per cent of the more than 7,000 participants. However, the 2020 Tokyo games (held in 2021) were the first gender-balanced Olympic Games in history, with nearly 49 per cent of the athletes being women.

1988

2021

Finally, we are getting SOMEWHERE!

It's been a long, hard road to have women's sport fully recognised at the Olympics. A lot of people have worked very hard to **achieve** that, and they're all standing on the shoulders of the **unsung** heroine of women's sport, Alice Milliat.

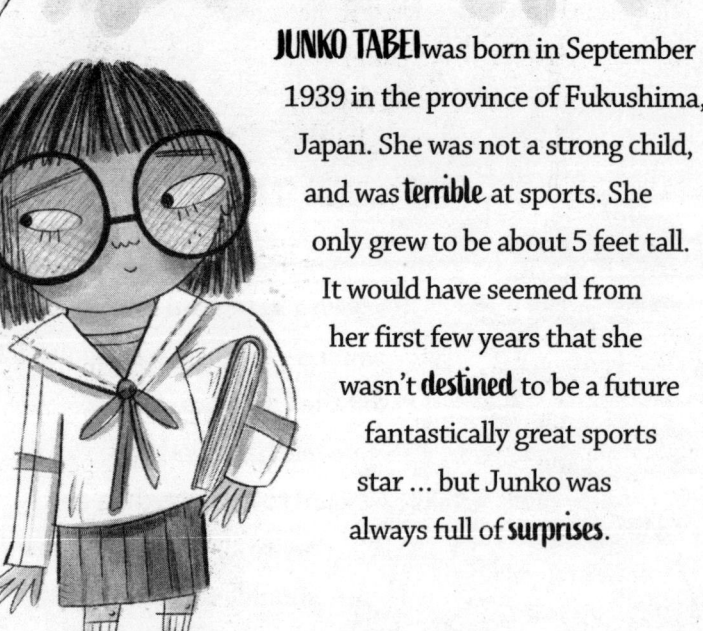

I'm on top of the WORLD!

There was no challenge too BIG, no mountain too HIGH for her to climb!

JUNKO TABEI

JUNKO TABEI was born in September 1939 in the province of Fukushima, Japan. She was not a strong child, and was **terrible** at sports. She only grew to be about 5 feet tall. It would have seemed from her first few years that she wasn't **destined** to be a future fantastically great sports star ... but Junko was always full of **surprises**.

When she was 10, Junko went on a school climbing trip to Mount Nasu, and **loved** it. Climbing suited her in a way that other sports didn't – it allowed her to spend time in nature, and to just **challenge** herself rather than compete against other people. It was a trip that would change her life.

"My initial sense was that it was not competitive, unlike other sports, at least not in a team-like manner. No matter how slow a person walked, they could reach the summit, one step at a time."

"When we reached the summit that day, I felt a joy of achievement that I had never experienced before."

Junko enjoyed the physical exertion and the **amazing** beauty of the views from the peak.

She knew she wanted to do it again.

71

Unfortunately, mountain climbing is an **expensive** hobby. Japan's economy was in a bad way after the Second World War, which meant people didn't have much money. Junko was one of seven children, so her family already had to worry about whether they could **afford** to feed everyone. Paying for mountain climbing lessons wasn't an option, so Junko was only able to climb a few times as a schoolchild.

Junko's Family

Junko climbing

Junko intended to become a **teacher**, so she went to university to study English and American literature. After graduating she joined several **climbing clubs**, but found they were all full of men. Although some Japanese women had started mountain climbing in the early part of the century, it was still very much a male-dominated hobby. But Junko loved climbing and she wasn't going to be put off. Some of the men were welcoming, but others **refused** to climb with her or suggested she'd only joined to find a husband. Junko didn't care, as long as she could **climb**.

CLIMBING ADVENTURE CLUB

NAME: Junko

LIKES: BIG MOUNTAINS

Bring me the MOUNTAINS, NOT a husband.

Before long she had climbed all the biggest mountains in Japan!

YES!

Around this time, Junko met a well-known mountaineer called Masanobu Tabei, who understood her **love** for mountains. Their first date was spent climbing Mount Tanigawa, a very **dangerous** peak! Junko's mother didn't approve of Masanobu because he didn't have a degree, but they got married anyway.

Masanobu Tabei*

Let's walk!

Together!

Our wedding!

Masanobu had a good job at
Honda, the car manufacturers, so he was
able to **support** his family. Unfortunately, not long
after they were married he lost four toes to frostbite
during an expedition to the Matterhorn, a large mountain
in the Alps. This made it more **difficult** for him to climb,
so in the future he would look after their two children
while Junko went on **expeditions**. This was unusual for a
Japanese man of his time – but the
Tabeis weren't a **usual** couple.

75

Junko decided to set up
a climbing group **just** for
women. So in 1969, she
started the Joshi-Tohan Club
(Women's Mountaineering Club)
which had the motto, 'Let's go on an overseas
expedition by ourselves'. But it took a **long time** to raise
enough money for an expedition. Junko worked long
hours as an **editor** for a science journal, and gave piano and
English lessons to make extra money.

In 1970, the Joshi-Tohan Club set off on their
first overseas expedition to the Nepalese mountain
Annapurna III. It was an **all-woman** expedition, except for
the male Sherpa, who would act as their guide. It was only
the second time an all-woman group had been allowed to
climb in Nepal – the first group had come to a tragic end
when four members were killed in an avalanche. Junko
and her team would have to be very **careful**.

MAP OF ANNAPURNA III

Annapurna III had only been climbed once before, from the north. The Joshi-Tohan expedition set off using a new route on the south side. It was a **difficult** and **dangerous** climb – but they did it! Despite the heavy snow, Junko and her team became the **first** female group (as well as the first Japanese group) to successfully climb the mountain. Unfortunately, when they got to the top the film in their camera broke because it was so **cold**!

Annapurna III

The camera is broken!

ticket to NEPAL

Junko **learned** a lot on Annapurna III. She had been brought up with the traditional Japanese values of politeness, quiet strength and self-reliance – but those traits could cause problems in the mountains. Some of her fellow climbers were reluctant to **admit** ignorance or **ask** for help when they were in trouble. Junko realised that if they wanted to climb safely and successfully, she couldn't be polite and quiet. She had to **speak up**, give her opinion and not worry about what other people thought.

"When we began the climb we were determined to only show each other our strong sides. When you are climbing a mountain, your life depends on the exact opposite. You can't be reserved and not say what you think or feel. You need to have a relationship where, when you're climbing, you can say, 'I need to go slower.'"

Back in Japan, she and her friends had a new target: **Mount Everest**. Junko applied for a permit to climb in 1971, but wasn't able to get a slot until spring 1975. It was a **long wait**, but she used the time to raise funds (money) for the expedition – and during that time, she and Masanobu had a daughter they named Noriko. She also had a son named Shinya.

NORIKO & SHINYA

The cost of the trip would be **huge**. She tried to get **sponsorship** but was told that Everest was no place for a woman, that it simply wouldn't be possible for her to do it, and that women should stay home with their children. The team members had to dig into their own **savings**, and Junko made some of their climbing gear herself, including making trousers out of old curtains. Finally, her team managed to get **funding** from a Japanese TV station and the newspaper *Yomiuri Shimbun*.

All set for Everest!

JUNKO'S DIARY: 4 May 1975

The 15 of us set off in a blaze of glory ... and all the attention was on us! Our plan was to follow the route used by Sir Edmund Hillary and Tenzing Norgay, the first men to reach the summit, the highest point. But unfortunately, things didn't start well ...

4th MAY

NEPAL

NEPAL 1975

Sugar f energy

ALL WOMEN

TRIP TO NEPAL

At half past midnight on 4 May, I was at Camp II. Me and my group were sleeping in tents pitched on a freezing, windswept peak 21,326 feet (ft) above **sea level**. By Everest standards, it was a safe spot. But I woke to the noise of a terrible, thunderous roar. Avalanche!

AVALANCHE!

Me and my four tentmates were hit by a wave of snow and ice that threw us down the slope in a tangle of bodies and equipment. It was terrifying. I found myself squashed by my friends' bodies, buried under snow. I remember having a vision of Noriko playing. Then I must have passed out.

I was told later that the Sherpa guides dug me out and found me unconscious. They also dug out my friends - saving us all from dying of suffocation. Amazingly, nobody had been killed. As soon as I knew everyone was alive, I was determined to continue.

I was the worst injured of the party, so battered and bruised that it took two days before I could walk properly. Several people argued that I should be airlifted out to hospital. But I refused. I couldn't abandon the expedition. I had learned on Annapurna III to be honest about needing help, but I was quite sure I was well enough to carry on.

DANGER

WATCH OUT!

Everest is a terribly dangerous place. Even if you're spared an avalanche, the cold and lack of oxygen can be deadly. There have been more than 300 recorded deaths on the mountain, and there are more than 200 human bodies on Everest now. Because of the cold, bodies that would rot away at sea level don't decompose. They can't be carried down again because it's too dangerous: more people would have to risk their lives to retrieve them. So they are left on the mountainside and are still there to this day.

We CAN DO this!

Me, determined ...

We had to dig out our supplies and oxygen from the snow. That was a blessing in disguise, as it gave me a little more time to recover. Once we had everything, we set off on our climb. We had no time to waste. Our food and oxygen supplies wouldn't last forever, and we were all suffering from the physical demands of the climb and living at high **altitude**.

Oww!

Noodles

As the team reached the top, we faced another problem. The plan had been to send two members of the expedition to the summit. But as the air was too thin to breathe, we realised that the climbers would need to be accompanied by a Sherpa carrying enough bottles of oxygen to get them up to the summit and down again.

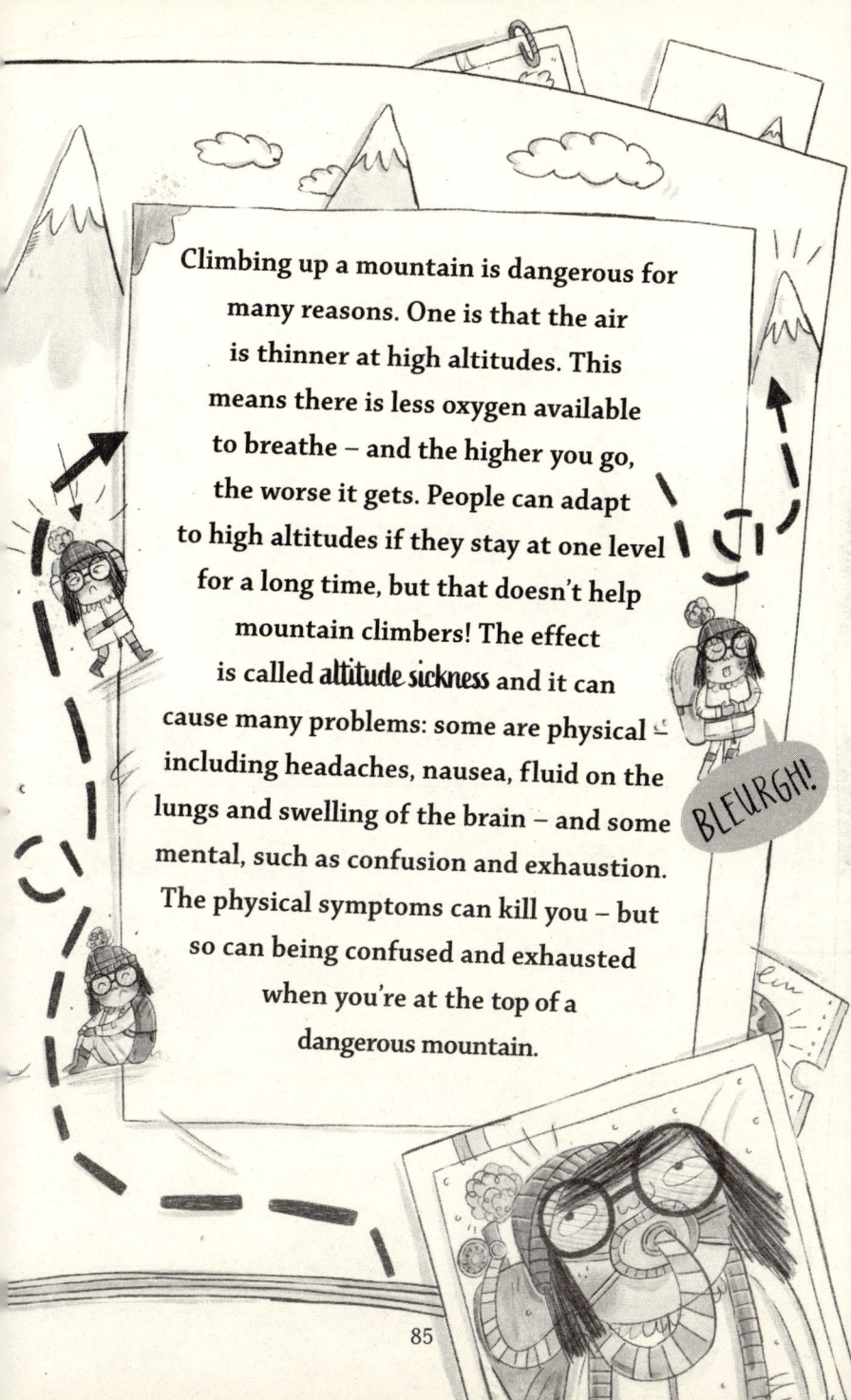

Climbing up a mountain is dangerous for many reasons. One is that the air is thinner at high altitudes. This means there is less oxygen available to breathe – and the higher you go, the worse it gets. People can adapt to high altitudes if they stay at one level for a long time, but that doesn't help mountain climbers! The effect is called altitude sickness and it can cause many problems: some are physical – including headaches, nausea, fluid on the lungs and swelling of the brain – and some mental, such as confusion and exhaustion. The physical symptoms can kill you – but so can being confused and exhausted when you're at the top of a dangerous mountain.

BLEURGH!

Unfortunately, the Sherpas, like the rest of us, were suffering from altitude sickness, and none of them could carry enough oxygen for two people. That's when we decided only one woman and one Sherpa could make the final **ascent**. Kindly, my wonderful team chose me and Sherpa Ang Tsering to do it.

I remember on the Annapurna III expedition, there had been jealousy and resentment from the team members who weren't chosen to reach the summit. I was worried this might happen again, but luckily I was proven wrong.

Whoo!

Go, Junko!

"We had already spent more than fifty days at more than **5,000 metres**; living in such a stark environment had begun to wear on us — we had been pushed to the far edge of **tiredness**. The unspoken thought that we shared was that if someone, **anyone**, could reach the summit, **then please, let them so** we can **go home.**"

It was a *terrifying climb.* At one point I had to crawl sideways along a thin ridge of ice, which was the scariest experience I've ever had. Just one tiny mistake, a slip or a fall, would mean death. I clambered on painful hands and bruised knees to the summit, and looked down past the clouds far below. It was 12.30 p.m. on 16 May 1975, and I'd done it. I was the first woman to reach the top of Everest, accompanied by the wonderful Sherpa, Ang Tsering.

"I felt **pure joy** as my thoughts registered: Here **is** the summit. I don't have to climb **any** more."

Junko was **famous**! There was a **parade** in her honour in Kathmandu, and the Japanese government honoured her. There was even a TV miniseries made about her! Junko did a lot of interviews, but she didn't like it. She preferred to be considered the thirty-sixth person to summit Everest, not the first woman.

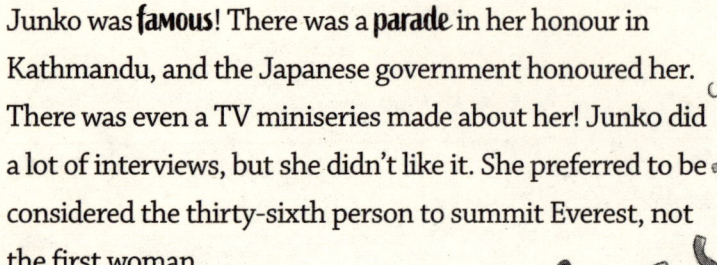

Lots of companies wanted to **sponsor** her next climb. But Junko didn't want to do that again.

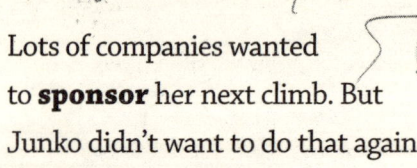

"If I accept sponsorship, then climbing the mountain is not my own experience. It's like working for the company."

She preferred to raise the money herself by doing public events, guiding mountain tours and teaching. Mountains were not her job, but her **joy**. For a long time, when filling out forms, Junko put her occupation as 'housewife', only later changing to '**mountaineer**'.

Junko kept on climbing. She became the first woman to complete the **Seven Summits Challenge**, climbing the highest mountain on each continent. She also set herself the personal goal of climbing the highest mountain in every country in the world! She didn't climb them all, but managed at least 70 of them.

Nobody has yet completed this challenge and probably nobody ever will. There are a lot of countries (close to 200), and wars and political problems often get in the way. It is also illegal to climb the highest mountain in Bhutan because of the spiritual beliefs of its people.

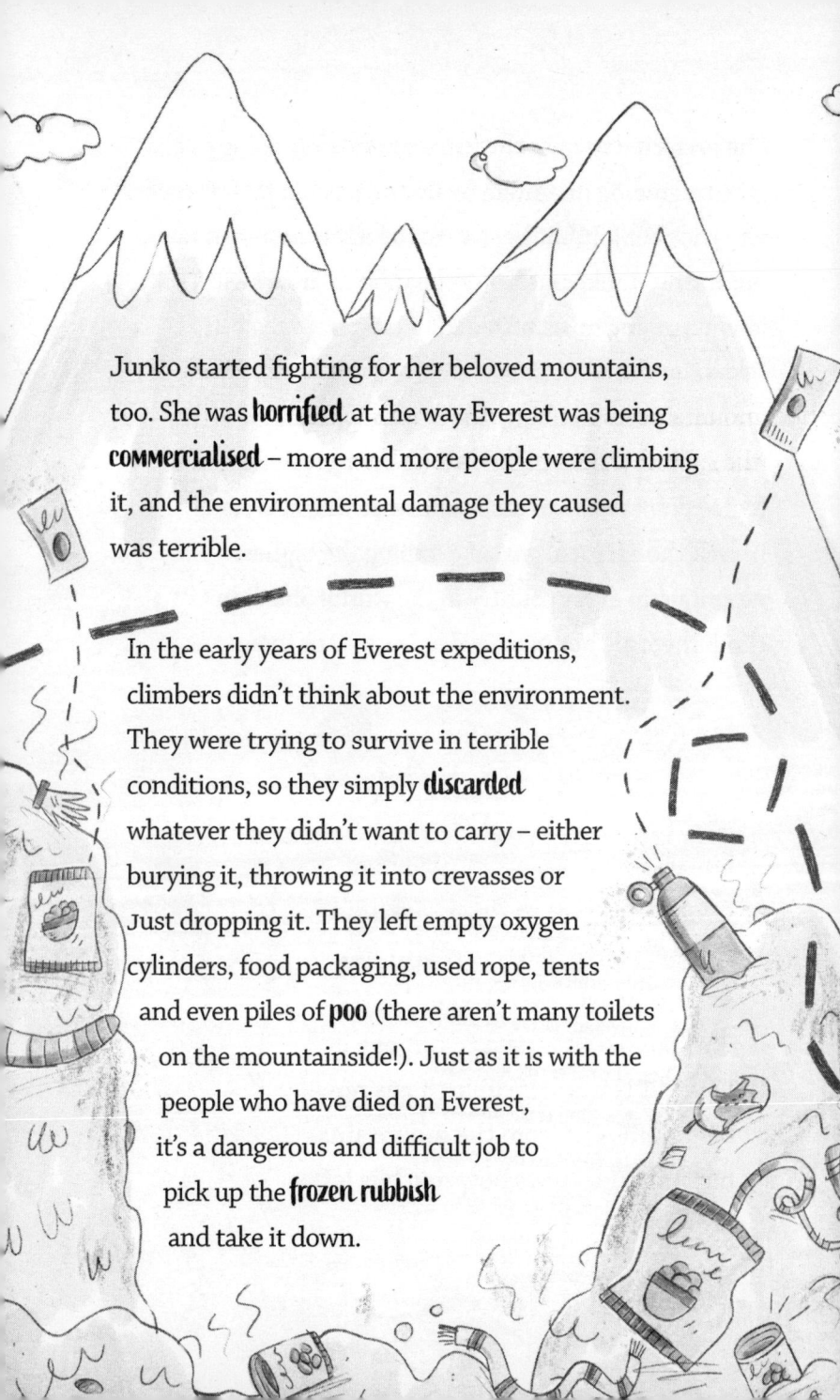

Junko started fighting for her beloved mountains, too. She was **horrified** at the way Everest was being **commercialised** – more and more people were climbing it, and the environmental damage they caused was terrible.

In the early years of Everest expeditions, climbers didn't think about the environment. They were trying to survive in terrible conditions, so they simply **discarded** whatever they didn't want to carry – either burying it, throwing it into crevasses or just dropping it. They left empty oxygen cylinders, food packaging, used rope, tents and even piles of **poo** (there aren't many toilets on the mountainside!). Just as it is with the people who have died on Everest, it's a dangerous and difficult job to pick up the **frozen rubbish** and take it down.

Junko went back to university, aged nearly 60, to do a postgraduate degree in environmental science, studying the impact of human waste on the Himalayas. She became director of the Himalayan Adventure Trust of Japan, working to preserve mountain environments, and led 'clean-up climbs' in Japan and the Himalayas, where mountaineers went on expeditions to clear the rubbish. Like a high-altitude litter pick!

Since Junko and people like her called attention to the problem, climbers have had to pay litter fees and carry rubbish down or be fined. Sherpas are also paid to remove it. Over 11 tonnes of rubbish has now been removed from the mountains, but nobody knows how much is left.

WOW!

Mt. Fuji

In 2012, Junko was diagnosed with stomach cancer. She kept on **climbing**, and even took an expedition of young people up Mount Fuji in July 2016. She died in October that year.

Junko leaves an amazing **legacy**. As well as writing seven books, she also has an asteroid and a mountain range on Pluto named after her.

Most importantly, Junko changed ideas of what women in Japan could or *should* do – because she changed her own ideas about what was **important**. She became a role model for women who want to do their own things and follow their dreams, and not worry about what anyone thinks they **should** do.

"If people want to call me 'that crazy mountain woman,' that's OK."

derartu TULU

Born in 1972, **Derartu Tulu** was raised in a small town called Bekoji in the middle of **Ethiopia**. It's a beautiful place with rich red soil and lots of vegetation, surrounded by mountains in the distance.

But it isn't a wealthy place. It has about 17,000 people, many of them living in single-room houses. There aren't any grand buildings or shiny sports facilities. Hardly anyone has a car. Most people still get around by horse or donkey – or on foot. *Especially* on foot. Because this small town is home to some of the world's **greatest** runners. And the first of those to make her mark on the world stage was Derartu.

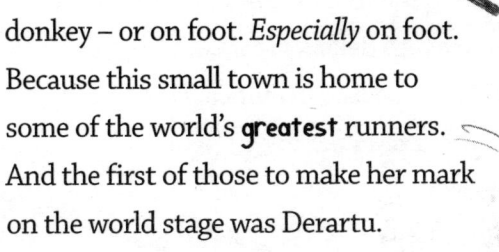

"Derartu used to practise on the field here every day. She used to help her mum AND do training ... When she was five or six we knew she was unusual ... She was a very strong, powerful girl."

Derartu trained with a **coach** named Sentayehu Eshetu, who had recently moved to Bekoji. He wasn't a highly trained sports coach, but he paid **attention**. He spotted Derartu's **gifts** and **encouraged** her to compete.

Derartu's parents weren't very pleased about her running at first. She had plenty to do looking after the family's cows! They worried that if she became **successful** she would leave home and they would lose her. The first time Derartu ran a race, she was given a dress as a prize for **winning** – and she hid it so her mum wouldn't know. The second time she ran, she got a glass **trophy**. She showed that to her mum.

Her parents allowed her to run after that.

Phewee ...

Bekoji didn't have **state-of-the-art** training facilities. But it's a good landscape for runners, with flat land surrounded by hills, allowing runners to train in all **conditions**. It is also positioned at a very high **altitude**.

BEKOJI

Bekoji is about 10,500 ft above sea level. The air is thin so high up because it has less oxygen. If you aren't used to such conditions, it makes it hard to exercise: each breath delivers less oxygen to your muscles than it would at sea level. This was a problem in the 1968 Olympics, held in Mexico City, which is 7,350 ft above sea level - nowhere near as high as Bekoji, but higher than many athletes were used to.

The RUNNER

MEXICO CITY

The athletes doing endurance events, such as long-distance running, found it much more difficult than normal - they just couldn't take in enough oxygen.

Looks hard!

When people regularly exercise at high altitudes, their bodies eventually adapt to get the oxygen they need. Those athletes produce more red blood cells, which lets their blood carry more oxygen. And it means when they go down to sea level, their muscles get more oxygen than people who have lower red blood cell counts - giving them an extra boost!

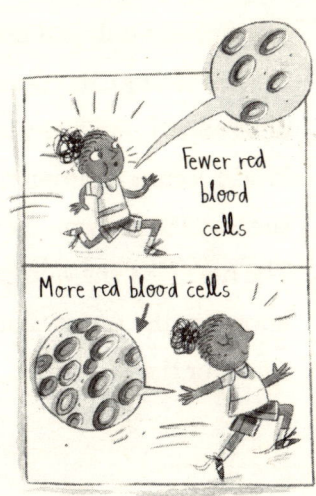

Fewer red blood cells

More red blood cells

Some athletes who usually live at low altitudes train at high altitudes in order to increase their red blood cells. The problem is, it's still much harder to run at high altitudes! So you can't do as much training.

The ideal situation for an athlete with enough funding might be to live at high altitude (for the red blood cells) but to train at low altitude (where you can keep going for longer) But that wasn't an option for Derartu - Bekoji was her home.

Derartu was only just over 5 ft tall and weighed about 7 stone (44 kg). But despite her size, she was strong and determined – and very fast! Her first **big victory** was at the World Junior Championships in Bulgaria in 1990, when she was 18. She won the **gold medal** in the 10,000 m race. The next year she won gold at the All-Africa Games (now known as the Africa Games) in Egypt, again for the 10,000 m.

Derartu Tulu

BULGARIA 1990

EGYPT 1991

But she needed to make her mark at the most famous event in the world: Derartu Tulu was going to the **Olympic Games**.

In 1992, the Olympics was held in Barcelona.
In the 10,000 m, Derartu and Elana Meyer (a white
South African runner) raced each other – for lap after
lap they were both way out in front of all the other
runners. It was a **nail-biting** race, often called one of
the most **thrilling** of all time. Just before the last lap,
Derartu overtook Elana Meyer and ran the last lap in an
amazing 64 seconds. (Each lap is 400 m. The world record
for the women's 400 m is 47.6 seconds – but that was set
by someone who hadn't just run 9,600 m beforehand!)
She won by a 30-metre margin.

Derartu waited at the finish line for Elana, and gave
her a **hug**. Then they joined hands and ran the lap of
honour together, each wearing their country's flag. At
this time, the cruel and racist South African system of
apartheid that oppressed Black people was at last
coming to its end. By running together,
hand in hand, Derartu Tulu and Elana
Meyer symbolised a new **hope**
and future for Africa.

472

1474

Derartu Tulu was not just an Olympic champion, she was the **first** Black African woman **ever** to win an Olympic gold medal.

Unfortunately, a knee injury put her out of competition for the next two years. Then she came back with a **bang** in the 1995 World Cross Country Championships, which was held in Durham, UK – but it didn't start well. The Ethiopian Athletics Federation **messed up** the travel arrangements, and the Ethiopian team took three days to get to Durham from Addis Ababa (Ethiopia's capital city). The team even had to spend a night at Athens airport without any food or water because the organisers didn't have enough money to pay for them to sleep in a hotel. The athletes arrived in Durham at 2 a.m. on the day of the first race, having had **hardly** any sleep. Yet, despite it all, Derartu still won **both** gold and silver medals!

But she was angry. When she got back home, Derartu led a **march** of more than 600 athletes from the stadium in Addis Ababa to demonstrate about how Ethiopian sport was being **badly** managed. Luckily, the government **listened**. They fired the people who were responsible for the mess up, and replaced them with officials whom Derartu recommended.

"Our athletics federation thought I was a troublemaker. But I had to stand up for my colleagues' rights. If I hadn't, nothing would ever have changed."

LISTEN to US!

LOOK after US!

BETTER MANAGE-MENT

FAIR PLAY for ETHIOPIAN SPORT

ETHIOPIA

Despite her wins at the 1995 Championships, things didn't go so well for a little while. Derartu had an accident at the 1996 World Cross Country Championships when her **shoe** came off (leaving her in fourth place), and then she suffered from an injury during the Olympic Games that year. Derartu decided to put her running career on **hold**. She used the money she'd earned to buy a hotel, and then, in 1998, she had a daughter, Tsion.

ARGH!

"In Barcelona, I was very young and did not always appreciate what was happening. Now I have a child and I'm very experienced. I know you have to enjoy these moments because life is not always this **good**."

DERARTU TULU HOTEL

104

·SYDNEY·

By now, Derartu felt ready to **restart** her racing
career. Looking after a baby meant that she
couldn't come back to racing immediately, but
when she did she was in **tip-top** shape!
She won gold for a second time in the 10,000 m
at the 2000 Sydney Olympics, famously
sprinting the whole last lap in an astounding
60 seconds and setting a new African and
Olympics **record**. That made her the **first**
woman to win a long-distance gold
in two separate Olympics! But she
wouldn't be the only one ...

60:00

WOW!

Bekoji's Superstars

Another woman soon won gold in the 10,000 m at two Olympic games - in Beijing in 2008 and in London in 2012. Her name was Tirunesh Dibaba - Derartu's cousin!

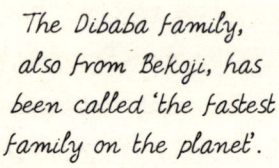

The Dibaba family, also from Bekoji, has been called 'the fastest family on the planet'.

Tirunesh Dibaba has won three Olympic gold medals. At the 2008 Beijing Olympics, she broke Derartu's Olympic record for the 10,000 m, and also won the 5,000 m. She won 10,000 m gold at the London Olympics in 2012. She also has five World Championship gold medals (and the record for youngest ever World Championship winner), and five World Cross Country golds, too.

Ejegayehu, her older sister, won silver in the 10,000 m in Athens 2004, beating Derartu into third place.

Their younger sister Genzebe won a World Championship gold in 2015, an Olympic silver in 2016 and a World Cross Country silver in 2017. She is also a five-time World Indoor Championship winner. At one point, she held four world records for track events - the most ever held by one person at the same time.

As well as being home to Derartu and the Dibaba family, Bekoji is the hometown of Kenenisa Bekele, one of the greatest distance runners of all time.

He has won three Olympic golds, five World Championship golds and eleven World Cross Country golds (and one silver!). His younger brother Tariku has an Olympic bronze. Also from Bekoji are Fatuma Roba - the first African woman to win an Olympic **marathon** gold, at Atlanta 1996 - and Tiki Gelana, who won gold for the marathon in London 2012.

All of those runners came from Bekoji, the little town in the Ethiopian highlands with the fastest runners in the world. And all of them were coached by Sentayehu Eshetu, perhaps the greatest coach of **all** time!

Derartu won the World Cross Country Championships for the third time in 2000. The next year, she won a World 10,000 m track title, the London Marathon and the Tokyo Marathon. She won several **important** half marathons over the next couple of years, and bronze in the 10,000 m at the 2004 Athens Olympics.

Derartu had another daughter in 2006, and it seemed as though her racing days were coming to an end. But in 2009, at the age of 37, Derartu had one last title to **claim** ... and one final rival to **beat**.

Go, Mum!

PAULA RADCLIFFE

For many years, Derartu and the British long-distance runner Paula Radcliffe were rivals. They were close to the same age and they raced each other frequently. Derartu often won, but not always, and usually the races were incredibly close. In the 1997 World Cross Country Championships, Derartu finished just two seconds in front of Paula to win gold! But Paula Radcliffe was the world record holder for fastest women's marathon runner – a record she set in 2003 that wasn't broken until 2019.

The two women were always in competition – and sometimes it boiled over. They weren't always nice about each other.

In 2009, Paula was 35. She'd already come first in the New York City Marathon three times. But now Derartu decided to run it as well. She hadn't won a title for several years and she had only ever won two marathons, London and Tokyo, both back in 2001.

The race was **on**! Paula and Derartu were in the lead, along with two other runners. But just over halfway, Paula started struggling. Her hamstring was hurting **badly**. Derartu could tell Paula had some kind of **injury**.

Derartu turned to her old rival. 'Come on,' she said. 'We can do it.'

Derartu ran **alongside** Paula over the next stretch to keep her going, and even waited when Paula slowed down on a hill, letting the other runners get **ahead** of her!

But Paula's injury meant she just couldn't keep up. So Derartu ran back to the people ahead of her. With a quarter of a mile left to go, she put on a **burst** of her old, amazing speed and flashed past the rest.

She was the **first** Ethiopian woman to win the New York City Marathon!

Paula came fourth, crying with pain as she limped over the **finish line**, and Derartu grabbed her in a hug.

"That's Derartu. She's always lovely like that."

PAULA

Derartu

Derartu continued to run well into her late thirties. Her last marathon finish was in Yokohama in 2011. She became interim **president** of the Ethiopian Athletics Federation in 2018, taking the position permanently in 2021.

She has been a huge success – and she's always **shared** that success with other people. Along with her race prize money, she was given land and rewards by her country for her **world-beating** achievements. She invested in businesses in Addis Ababa, and always helps family and friends from home.

YOKOHAMA 2011

I will speak up for Ethiopian sport.

"If the neighbours have problems, they ask, and Derartu will help. Even if they don't ask, she can see and will help. That's how she is."

MARTA VIEIRA DA SILVA

The small town girl who became a **BIG** football **STAR!**

Marta Vieira da Silva is often referred to as the **greatest** woman footballer of all time. With **amazing** dribbling skills and express-train speed, she has been named **FIFA** World Player of the Year six times, she's Brazil's top international goalscorer and she holds the **world record** for the most goals scored in both the men's and women's World Cup.

But success didn't come easily ...

Marta was born in 1986 in Dois Riachos, a town in the north-east of Brazil. It's a very poor place with a population of about 12,000 people, but with little work available. Her father, a hairdresser, left her mother when Marta was just a baby. It was very difficult for her mother to raise four children alone and they grew up in **poverty**.

"We didn't have enough money even to buy a football. If my mum had done that we would have gone without food."

Marta **loved** to play football, so much so she would stuff newspapers into hand-me-down shoes to make them fit – then played football in the streets with local boys. If ever they couldn't find a ball, they would bundle up lots of plastic bags into a makeshift ball. Some people will do **anything** to play football!

The problem was, girls in Brazil weren't **supposed** to play football. Until 1979, it had been forbidden by Brazilian law for women to play football at all! Once, an amateur (non-professional) football coach in Manaus put a girl in his team, and the Ministry of Education sent someone to put a **stop** to it. The government eventually scrapped the law in 1979, but people's attitudes towards women's football have taken a lot longer to **change**.

"My biggest battle was to fight against **prejudice**. Some kids didn't like the idea of a girl playing ... But, at the same time, I was never the last pick when they were choosing teams, so that was a sign that I was on the right path."

Poor Marta didn't even have support from her own family. Her older brother didn't want her to play because of the insults he knew she'd suffer. But Marta **kept** playing. She developed her ball skills, and learned to be tough – **physically** and **mentally** – as well as fast. Eventually, she found a five-a-side indoor team who let her join their team – as their **only** girl.

"I played in the local championship for two years, until another team said that they would withdraw from the tournament if I continued to play. There was a huge controversy and the championship organiser thought it would be better if I didn't **play** any more."

BRAZIL

When Marta was 14, friends sent word that one of the **big** Rio de Janeiro clubs, Vasco da Gama, was having **try-outs** for a women's team. Marta got on the bus alone. The 1,000-mile journey took her three days, but once she'd arrived, Marta's skill was **obvious**, as was her **determination**.

Bye!

DOIS RIACHOS

Almost there!

1000 miles...

She's good!

RIO de JANEIRO

VASCO DA GAMA CLUB

Marta put her all into the try-outs. She'd even brought **new** boots for the occasion! And it paid off. After the first day of the trials, the club took Marta on. Marta couldn't **believe** it – this was the **moment** she'd been working towards! She was voted the **best** player of her first Brazilian tournament. And she was still only 15.

Marta hoped this was when her football career was going to take off and started sending money home to her mother. But women's football was, and still is, badly **underfunded** in Brazil. Within three years, Vasco had scrapped its women's team. But Marta wasn't going to be **beaten**. She kept trying, playing for various teams in tiny towns – until she was picked for the 2003 Women's World Cup squad aged just 17.

The great Brazilian player Pelé also made his World Cup debut at 17. A lot of people who watched Marta thought that was a sign for how great she would become. Brazil only reached the quarter-finals, but she was the **talk** of the **tournament**.

MARTA aged 17

PELÉ aged 17

Women's World Cup
The first FIFA Women's World Cup was held in 1991, and there has been a women's football tournament at the Olympics since 1996.

However, there is a big difference between the way women's football and men's football are treated. In the 2018 men's World Cup, 32 teams competed for £315 million in prize money. But at the women's World Cup in 2019, the total prize money awarded to all participating teams was just £24 million – and that was double what they had received at the previous World Cup in 2015.

ERM?

The excuse for this difference is that men's football attracts more viewers and makes more money from advertising. But far more money is put into men's sport in the first place, meaning that it gets more viewers, more worldwide interest and more financial support. When women's football is properly publicised, people do watch: more than 1.1 billion people tuned in to watch the 2019 women's World Cup. That's a lot! Maybe if FIFA started putting more money into women's football then they would get a lot more out of it!

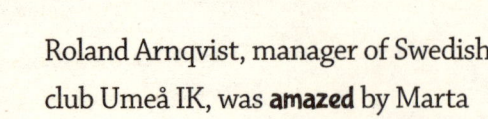

Roland Arnqvist, manager of Swedish club Umeå IK, was **amazed** by Marta and wanted her to come and play for his club. But there was a problem. Getting in touch with Marta was **almost** impossible, as she didn't have an **agent** or a telephone, and she didn't even speak any English! Luckily, Arnqvist was very **determined** and after two months he finally tracked her down.

When Marta got the **offer** she couldn't believe it – to start with she thought it was a joke! But she signed with the team. This made her the **first** Brazilian woman to play **professionally** in Europe. The Brazilian team coach René Simões thought it was her only choice, saying, "The few sides we have are not professional enough ... If you want to reach the top in women's football, you have to play in a top league, like those in Europe."

Marta encountered lots of challenges by moving to a new country. One of them was getting used to the **temperature** in Sweden. Marta went from living in a hot, dusty town in Brazil to a country less than 200 miles from the Arctic Circle. It was desperately **cold**!

"The cold was a challenge. I went from 35 degrees every day in Brazil to a place where it reaches minus 22 degrees in the winter. But my life has always been about breaking barriers. I saw everything as a challenge."

There was also the **language barrier**. Marta could not speak Swedish! She insisted that as part of her **contract**, the club must pay for her to have **language lessons**. She worked hard and soon learned to speak **fluently**, partly by watching a lot of Swedish TV. In time, she saw Sweden as her second home.

Kall is Swedish for cold!

Marta performed spectacularly for the club. She led Umeå IK to the league **championship** four times, becoming the **best-paid** female footballer in Sweden, and scoring the most goals in the league season after season. She was named FIFA World Player of the Year every year from 2006 to 2010.

For Umeå!

Marta's agent (now she'd got one!) reflected on how she had to leave Brazil to find success:

"Football is a religion here, but this country has not been there for Marta. She'd never be recognised as one of the best players in the world if she had stayed in Brazil. Who's the most awarded football player in the world? It's a woman – but that answer is a bit awkward in Brazil."

In 2007, Marta played for the Brazilian women's team to beat the USA in the final of the Pan American Games. Pelé himself called her **'Pelé in skirts'**, and called to **congratulate** her.

AMAZING!

On the day she was named **FIFA World Player of the Year** for the fourth time in 2009, she announced she was **transferring** to Los Angeles Sol in America . The first of many moves …

FIFA Player of the Year

POSTCARD

"For me, the most important thing is to be in a place where the best players in the world are playing, and this is what they are trying to do here. The American League is being considered one of the best in the world, so I had to come now."

Minha Casa
Dois Riachos
BRAZIL!

BOARDING CARD
RIO DE JANEIRO
LOS ANGELES

SEAT
2B

WELCOME
TO THE USA

POSTCARD

What a few seasons I've had in the USA! I might have been the league's top scorer but that hasn't stopped LA Sol going out of business, or the next club I played for. It's deeply frustrating that women's football is SO badly funded! I made my mark though, just wait until you see my awards!

Minha Casa
Dois Riachos
BRAZIL!

I can barely keep up with the ball! I'm back in Sweden, again. This time, the team at Orlando Pride in Florida, USA needs my skills!

Minha Casa

Dois Riachos

BRAZIL!

Marta played in the 2011 Women's World Cup, where Brazil went out in the quarter-finals, but was still the **second-highest** goalscorer. Her fourth World Cup in 2015 made her the all-time top scorer of the women's tournament with a total of 15 goals.

BRAZIL

MARTA VIEIRA DA SILVA

TIME TO SCORE 15 GOALS

2nd HIGHEST GOALSCORER
2011

MARTA!

WOMEN'S WORLD CUP LEGENDS STICKERS!!

CUP LEGENDS

In the 2019 World Cup, she became the **first player** – male or female – to score at five FIFA World Cup tournaments. In the next match, she became the outright **leading** goalscorer at any World Cup, with 17 goals in total.

"The feeling is joyful. Not only for breaking the record but for being able to represent women in doing so. We are trying to show how women can play any type of role ... and not only in sport. This is a struggle for equality across the board."

Unfortunately, the Brazilian team were **beaten** by France in the quarter-finals. Marta cares **passionately** about women's football, especially in her home country of Brazil where women's teams have so little **support**. So when her team lost to France, Marta made an emotional speech, begging home fans to pay more **attention** and to get involved with women's football. She knew that the survival of the women's game in Brazil depended on the next generation of players.

Marta also played in five Olympic tournaments for Brazil, twice winning silver. In the 2020 Tokyo Olympics, she became the first player ever to score in five Olympics in a row. She scored twice, but gave up a chance to make it a hat-trick by stepping aside to let a teammate take a **penalty**.

"There's no vanity here, we're a team."

She became a United Nations (UN) Goodwill Ambassador and Sustainable Development Goals advocate.

· UN WOMEN ·

Marta is a **record-breaking** player, one who electrified everyone who watched her play. More than that, she has fought for women's sports, and helped bring women's football into the **spotlight** – where it should be!

With more being done for fair pay and women's football finally getting the coverage it deserves, it's fair to say Marta had a small role to play in this and her **legacy** won't be forgotten.

Believe in yourself and trust yourself because if you don't believe in yourself, NO ONE ELSE WILL!

What people say about Marta ...

"It's definitely better to be on her team than playing against her. That's terrifying."

Ali Riley, former Umeå teammate

Meus amigos

"She's electric, with an array of moves that can make foes look like you've never played soccer before."

Mia Hamm, US champion footballer

"If a defender 'gives' Marta one side, she explodes past them right through it. How do you say 'see ya sucker!' in Portuguese?"

Christen Press, former Tyresö teammate

"You are much more than a football player. You help build a better world with your talent, in which women gain more space."

Pelé

"I never saw Pelé but I have seen Marta."
Banner at 2007 Pan American Games in Rio de Janeiro

133

ELLIE SIMMONDS

THE WOMAN WHO WINS IN THE WATER AND OUT OF IT!

TEAM GB

ELEANOR MAY SIMMONDS (known as Ellie) is a super swimmer who's been **making waves** since she was born. Her motto is "Work hard and believe in yourself". And she's certainly lived up to it.

Ellie was born in Walsall, in the West Midlands of the UK, in 1994. She was born with a condition known as **achondroplasia**, which is sometimes called dwarfism.

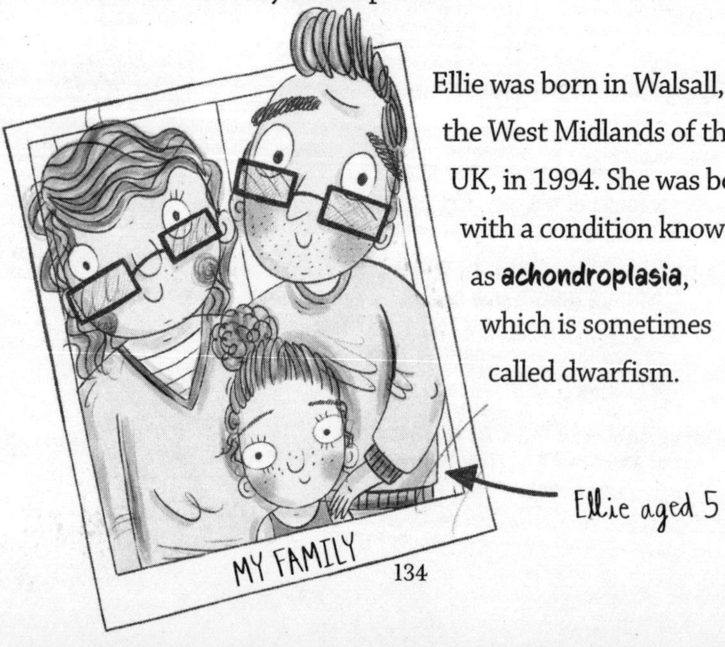

Ellie aged 5

MY FAMILY

134

People with achondroplasia are short, often around 4 feet tall as adults, with short limbs. Children often have less muscle development which makes it hard for them to walk, and they can suffer from other health problems because of it.

Ellie became interested in swimming when she was only five years old. Her parents took her to local pools to give her **confidence** in the water. It didn't take long! Soon she joined a swimming club, and her **talent** quickly became obvious.

When Ellie was nine, she watched the 2004 Athens Paralympics, and saw an incredible race by the swimmer Nyree Kindred (then Nyree Lewis). In that moment, Ellie knew she wanted to pursue swimming as a **career**.

THE PARALYMPIC GAMES

Formal sports clubs and events for people with disabilities have been around since at least 1888, when a sports club for deaf people was set up in Berlin, Germany.

After the Second World War, a German-Jewish refugee called Dr Ludwig Guttmann was working as the director of Stoke Mandeville's spinal cord injury unit in the U.K. He had been using sport as a way to help his patients and to give them exercise and fun. On the first day of the 1948 Olympic Games, Dr Guttmann set up a sports competition for British war veterans with spinal injuries.

It was called the Stoke Mandeville Games, and involved 16 British servicemen and women in an archery competition.

In 1952, Dutch veterans took part, and the games were renamed the International Stoke Mandeville games. They are considered the start of what would become the Paralympics.

The first official Paralympic games were held in Rome in 1960. There were 400 athletes competing from 23 countries - all were wheelchair users, but no longer had to be war veterans. Then in 1976, the competition was opened to athletes with other disabilities, and it grew to include athletes from 41 countries. That same year, the Winter Paralympics were introduced.

In 1988, for the first time, the Paralympics were held directly after the Olympics and in the same host city. Now the Paralympic and Olympic Committees work together. The Paralympic games are becoming more popular every time, and include more and more categories for disabled athletes.

Ellie watched Nyree win the gold medal. She was **gripped** – she didn't even know how old you had to be to compete in a race like that. All she knew was that she wanted to enter a Paralympics herself, and to win her own gold medal!

Nyree Kindred (then Nyree Lewis) is a Welsh swimmer with cerebral palsy, which is a condition that affects your movement and coordination. She has competed in four Paralympics and has won ten medals. She is married to Sascha Kindred, who is also a British Paralympic gold-medal-winning swimmer!

Ellie was determined to achieve her goal – and when her family saw her talent and drive, they were ready to help! When she was 11, she and her mother made the **big** decision to move to Swansea in Wales. There was a state-of-the-art swimming pool there that Ellie could use, and a **brilliant** coach named Billy Pye who agreed to train her. But the rest of the family, including her four older siblings, had to stay behind. Ellie missed her family, but would go back at weekends to visit. It was an unusual and sometimes difficult arrangement, but the family agreed Ellie was such an **amazing** swimmer, they'd be wasting her skills if they didn't go for it.

Thankfully, the move was worth it. Ellie was selected to compete at the 2008 Summer Paralympic Games in Beijing, China. Aged only 13 years old, she raced in five events and won **gold medals** in 100 metres (m) and 400 m freestyle. She was the **youngest** British athlete to compete, and the second youngest British Paralympian **ever** to win a medal.

GOOD LUCK!

WALSALL

WALES

SWANSEA

139

ENGLAND

ELLIE'S SCRAPBOOK

Ellie became a national hero. She won the BBC Young Sports Personality of the Year Award in 2008, which is given when a person has done something amazing for their sport that year. She was also given an award called a Member of the Order of the British Empire (**MBE**). Not many people get these, and it means you have done something very special.

Ellie was awarded her MBE by Queen Elizabeth II in 2009, becoming the youngest person ever to receive the honour. When she went to Buckingham Palace to receive her medal, her parents and grandmother came with her. Ellie said her one hope was that they wouldn't cry, because that would be embarrassing!

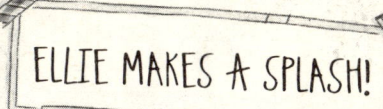

ELLIE MAKES A SPLASH!

And she was only just getting started. That year, she won six golds and a silver at the International Paralympics Committee (IPC) Swimming World Championships Short Course in Rio de Janeiro.

I won!

The next year, she won four gold, one silver and one bronze medal at the 2010 IPC Swimming World Championships in Eindhoven, in the Netherlands.

At the 2011 IPC Swimming European Championships in Berlin, Ellie took two gold, one silver and one bronze medal.

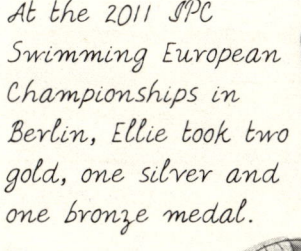

LONDON 2012

In 2012, the Olympic and Paralympic Games came to London. By then Ellie was such a **star** that she was one of the '**poster girls**' for the Paralympics, with a huge picture of her on the side of one of the buildings facing the Olympic Park. The **pressure** to win in her home Paralympics was **immense**, and Ellie felt nervous. Would she be able to live up to the expectations?

Go, Ellie!

DEEP END

143

Of course she would!

As nervous as she was, Ellie couldn't **wait** to perform in the sport she **loved**. She won a gold medal in the 400 m freestyle for the second Paralympic Games running – and even knocked five seconds **off** the world record time. But her successes weren't over yet. Ellie managed to set another world record in the qualifying round for the 200 m individual medley – and then broke it that **very** same evening in the final! Overall she won two gold medals, along with a silver and a bronze. She was a **star**!

As a **tribute** to the UK Olympian and Paralympian gold medallists in 2012, Royal Mail (the UK's postal service) decided to paint some of their red postboxes **gold**. Ellie has a gold postbox in her name in Walsall, where she was born, **and** one in Swansea, where she trained! She also appeared on a stamp to honour her **achievement**. Even more importantly, she was awarded an Order of the British Empire (**OBE**) to congratulate her for all her work in Paralympic sport. An OBE is an even **higher honour** than her previous MBE!

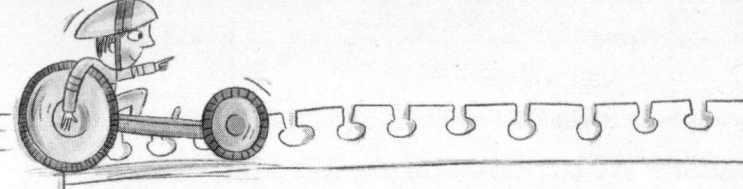

The word 'Paralympic' was invented to combine 'Olympic' and 'paraplegic' (which means paralysis of the lower half of the body). This was because the competition was originally just for wheelchair users. But when the Games got bigger and athletes with other disabilities joined in, they needed a name that would include everyone. Luckily, there is a Greek word para that means 'alongside' (like parallel lines). So now the word 'Paralympic' officially means that the Paralympic Games exist 'alongside' the Olympics.

To make the competition fair, the Paralympic Games have categories for people with all kinds of disabilities. There are 10 main categories, including people of short stature (such as Ellie) as well as those who have disabilities relating to their vision, their muscles and their brains. The Paralympics show the huge range of what people with disabilities can do, from playing rugby in a wheelchair to blind sprinting.

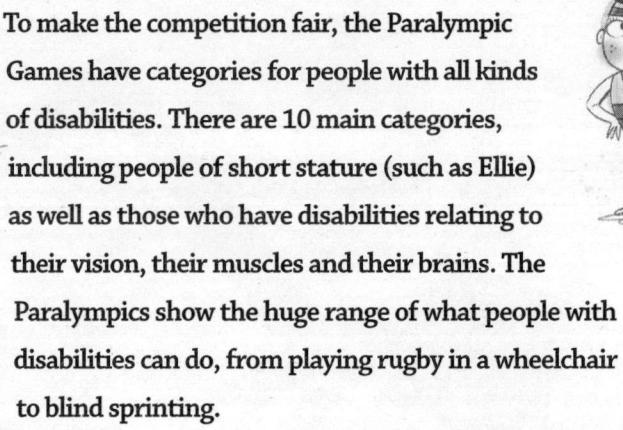

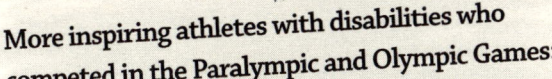
More inspiring athletes with disabilities who competed in the Paralympic and Olympic Games:

SARAH STOREY

British swimmer and cyclist Sarah Storey was born without a functioning left hand. She is the most **decorated** (most medals) female Paralympian in the world for cycling and swimming. She was made a **Dame** for her services to Paralympic sport in 2012.

ZIPORA RUBIN-ROSENBAUM

Zipora Rubin-Rosenbaum was born in Israel in 1946. After a childhood illness, Zipora was left unable to walk. She became **determined** to push her body to do new things, first trying to climb trees with other children and then in training sessions. She competed in her first Paralympics in 1964 and has won over 30 medals in athletics, swimming, javelin, table tennis and wheelchair basketball. That's a **lot** of sports!

ILDIKÓ REJTŐ

Hungarian fencer Ildikó Rejtő was born deaf. When she started fencing, her coaches used to hold up pieces of paper with instructions. She **competed** in five Olympics and **won** seven medals overall, including two gold.

Ellie seemed to be going from **strength** to **strength**. She won three gold medals and one bronze at the 2013 IPC Swimming World Championships in Montreal, Canada. And since 2008, Ellie had won every 400 m **freestyle** at either a World Championships or a Paralympic Games. But at the 2015 World Championships in Glasgow, Scotland, she **lost** to Ukraine's Yelyzaveta Mereshko. It was an exciting final, but she had to be content with silver.

The next Paralympics was held in Rio de Janeiro in 2016, but it wasn't a happy time for Ellie. She didn't have her usual **coach**, Billy Pye, as he had gone to work in China. And sadly there was a culture of bullying among some of the staff on the coaching team, who said cruel and **upsetting** things to the swimmers. Ellie was **devastated**. She had never been bullied for her dwarfism as a child, and it was horrible for her to face it now. Especially from people who were supposed to be on her **side**.

You might think professional athletes are all **strong** and **confident**. But they are often very **young**, far away from home, being put under huge **pressure** and enduring

gruelling training regimes. And it can be very difficult for them to speak up against older, experienced people – especially if they're **afraid** that speaking up might mean they don't get picked for a team.

But Ellie was **brave**, and she did speak out about her bad experience. She hoped that by talking about what she had gone through might mean no other Paralympic swimmer would face bullying from the staff. In total, 13 of the swimmers at Rio complained about bullying, and British Swimming had to make a **formal** apology for their treatment.

Even though she was very unhappy in Rio, Ellie still performed at the top of her game. She won her fifth Paralympic gold and set another world record in the 200 m **individual medley**. She also won a bronze in the 400 m freestyle. She was able to do it with grim determination because she believed the Paralympics was something **special**, and knew that performing in front of a big crowd would give her that extra **oomph**.

But Ellie never watches replays of her races in Rio. The memories are too bad.

my travels

After Ellie's negative experience, she wasn't even sure if she wanted to swim anymore. She had **dedicated** so much of her life to sport, maybe it was time to find out what else the world had to **offer**. So she decided to take a year out, and spent most of her time travelling. She went to China, Australia, South Africa and America, mostly on her own, and was able to think about what she really wanted from life. Taking time for herself helped her to **rediscover** her love of swimming.

welcome to AUSTRALIA

Ellie was reunited with her coach Billy Pye after her break. She enjoyed her **return** to swimming, but decided to **retire** aged 26 after the Tokyo 2020 Paralympics (held in 2021 due to COVID-19), when she had the **honour** of being the British team's **flagbearer**.

"I don't think I could go for another three years. I'm leaving it at the right time. I love it, I've absolutely had a wonderful competition and I've loved every minute of it."

Now Ellie devotes a lot of her time to **charity** work, in particular helping young people get into sport and swimming. She also works with **Water Aid**, is a **patron** of the Dwarf Sports Association, and is a Girl Guide leader. She has even written a series of books for children, based around her love of **baking**! Ellie says "Work hard and believe in yourself" – and that's exactly what she's done. Ellie has done so much to bring much-needed **respect** and **attention** to Paralympic sport and athletes, and in doing so has inspired many others to compete and have a go at sports they might not have tried before.

Ellie with WATER AID in UGANDA

DWARF SPORTS ASSOCIATION

Ellie Simmonds

"I'm just small. I can do everything everyone else can do. If I wasn't small I wouldn't have gone to the Paralympics. My philosophy is that there is no point in being sad or hating who you are. I just embrace every day as it comes and try to live the best I can."

gold medal.

S✦mone B✦les

Probably the greatest gymnast who's ever lived!

Simone Biles may be the **greatest** gymnast of all time. That's a big claim – but it's one made by other **incredible** gymnasts. The Romanian Olympic star Nadia Comăneci even called her 'one of a kind'. And when you read her story, you'll probably agree!

Simone was born in 1997 in Ohio, USA. She was one of four children but, sadly, her mother struggled to care for her and her siblings, and the children often had to live with other families – a system known as **foster care**. When Simone was three, her grandparents invited her to come and live with them, and they officially **adopted** her a few years later.

Not long after, Simone had her first taste of **gymnastics** while on a trip from day-care. The instructors saw immediately that she had talent, and said she should keep it up! Her grandparents enrolled her in a class, and by the age of eight, she was training with an artistic gymnastics coach called Aimee Boorman.

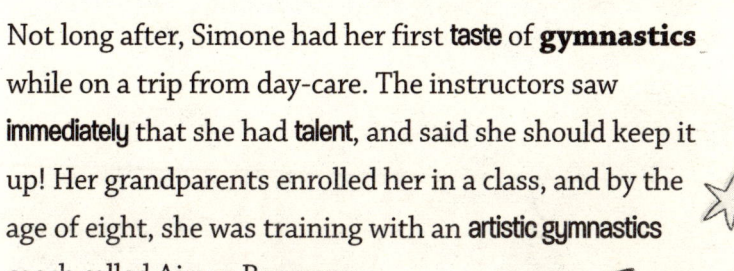

GREAT!

In artistic gymnastics, athletes perform short routines on different pieces of gym equipment, such as a vault or a beam. Routines must show grace and precision as well as strength. For women the events are:

UNEVEN BARS

VAULT

BALANCE BEAM

FLOOR EXERCISES

In the Olympics and World Championships, gymnasts compete as part of a national team, as well as individually for the all-around title.

By the time she was only 14, Simone's career as a top-level gymnastist had begun. She competed at the 2011 American Classic event, and she came first in the vault!

Some of the **acrobatic** elements of gymnastics are easier for girls who are small and light. As a result, in the 1970s the top gymnasts were getting younger and younger. Nadia Comăneci (the Romanian gymnast) was only 14 when she received a 'perfect 10' score at the 1976 Olympics. But the physical and mental demands of the sport were huge, and there was pressure for the gymnasts to become dangerously thin when they should have been growing. Thankfully, the minimum age for international competitions was raised to 16 years old, allowing women to compete for longer, and putting more value on their strength along with grace and precision. That was perfect for Simone, who is both strong and graceful!

Nadia

Over the next two years, she did so well that she was **selected** for the US Junior National Team. Then in 2013, one of the gymnasts on the senior team was injured and couldn't compete in the American Cup. Simone was chosen to replace her! She performed **brilliantly** and finished second in the competition after falling off the beam. She competed in several other events that year, including an **international** meet where she won three titles but only came second in the all-around title because of a fall off the **uneven bars**. Unfortunately, in her next competition – the 2013 US Classic – she didn't perform well, falling several times and twisting her ankle.

Whoo!

wobble   wobble

OUCH!

Simone was a good gymnast, but she knew she could be **much** better. She had the talent, but she was also **anxious** and did not have the confidence she needed. Luckily, Simone had a supportive family, and her grandfather reached out to a renowned sports **psychologist** called Robert Andrews. He spent time talking to Simone and **helped** her with her **anxiety**. You might think that someone who can master dangerous, difficult skills and compete at a national level would be confident already, but a lot of people are **less confident** than they seem. Simone's anxiety meant that she put too much **pressure** on herself and tried too hard, leading to mistakes.

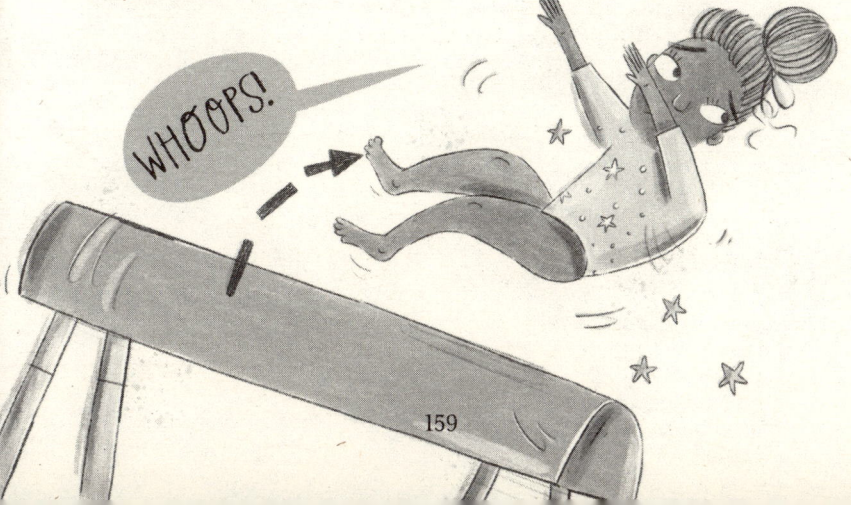

SIMONE'S DIARY:

I ♥ GYMNASTICS!

I was so worried that my anxiety would stop me from being a great gymnast. But Robert changed all that. He showed me that confidence is something that you can develop, and helped me to relax and enjoy gymnastics again.

"I had to convince her to take her foot off the gas, and enjoy the game again. She was so stoic at meets. It didn't look like she was having fun. Once she began interjecting that Simone smile into her floor routine, the fans and judges started smiling, too."

TENSE

Tah-dah!

Lots of gymnasts still feel afraid to ask for support when they have **mental health** problems because they think it makes them weak.

I'm a champion!

But I knew that asking for help would make me stronger. I became a champion because I was ready to get the help I needed. Finding ways to ease my anxiety made me feel better and happier - and it worked magic for my gymnastics too.

I became national all-around champion at the 2013 USA Gymnastics National Championships. I was also selected for the US national team, and won the 2013 World Artistic Gymnastics Competition, where I had a skill named after me for the first time! I was the first Black American woman to win the world all-around title. Then I won it again the next year, and again in 2015, making me the first woman ever to win three consecutive all-around titles.

THE BILES on the floor!

Simone's first Olympics was Rio de Janeiro in 2016 when she was 19. She was the only US gymnast to compete in the **final** of all four events, and she won a **spectacular** four gold medals. Her performance was so **amazing** that Team USA chose her for the honour of carrying the US flag at the closing ceremony.

But gymnastics was a gruelling sport, and Simone decided she needed some time off. She took a **break** from competition in 2017, and used the time to write a bestselling autobiography. She wanted to inspire other people to chase their dreams, just as she had done.

Courage
to
Soar

Simone Biles

Simone also appeared on the US TV show *Dancing with the Stars*. (She came **fourth**. You can't win 'em all, even if you're Simone Biles!)

She returned to competition in 2018. It was a difficult time for her because she had recently **spoken out** against a doctor on her sports team who had been doing things to hurt her. He had also hurt a lot of other gymnasts. It is not easy to talk about events that have upset you, but Simone was **brave**. By telling people what had happened, she made sure the doctor could not hurt anyone else.

The World Championships didn't start well for her either
– she had to go to hospital the night before with stomach
pains. But she went back to work the next morning – and
she had something special to show. Simone had been
working on a new vault.

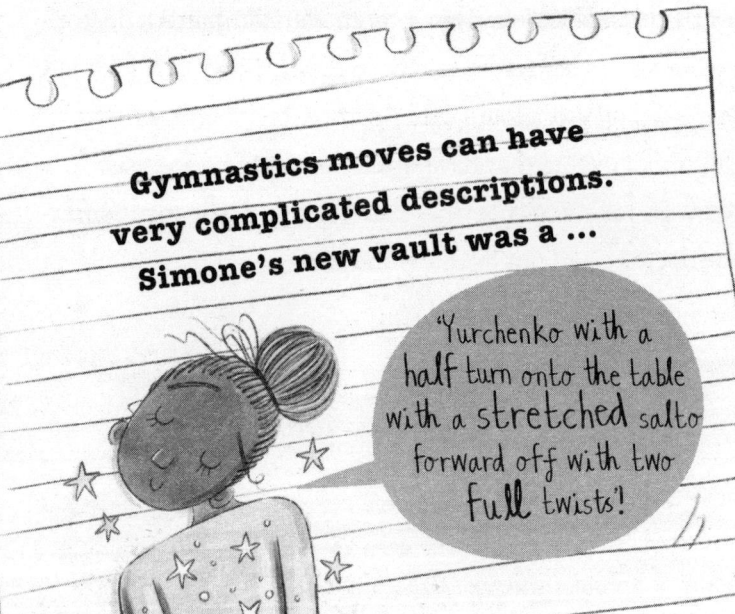

Gymnastics moves can have very complicated descriptions. Simone's new vault was a ...

'Yurchenko with a half turn onto the table with a stretched salto forward off with two full twists'!

The International Gymnastics Federation names skills after gymnasts – but only if they perform them successfully at a major international competition.

Simone completed the vault successfully, meaning it was officially 'the Biles'. It was given one of the highest difficulty ratings (6.4) because of the **power** it requires and the precision that is needed in order to land perfectly. This rating made the Biles vault equal first for the **most difficult** women's vault ever completed.

Gymnasts get two scores:

One for execution (how well they perform) and one for difficulty. These two scores are then added together to give an overall score. A difficulty score over 6.0 on any event is good. Simone's routines involved so many high-scoring skills that it was almost impossible for anyone else to catch up. So far, she is the only woman who has ever performed the Biles vault.

Simone's ability to do these difficult moves brought her **incredible** success. She won a fourth World all-around title, setting a new **world record** for women, and a thirteenth World gold medal, setting a new world record for women or men.

At the 2019 World Championships, Simone brought out two more new **skills**: the Biles II floor exercise – a triple-twisting double-tucked backflip (her second named floor exercise move) – and the Biles on the **balance beam** – a double-twisting double-tucked somersault dismount. The Biles II floor exercise was the highest-rated skill across all apparatuses in Women's Artistic Gymnastics.

Wow!

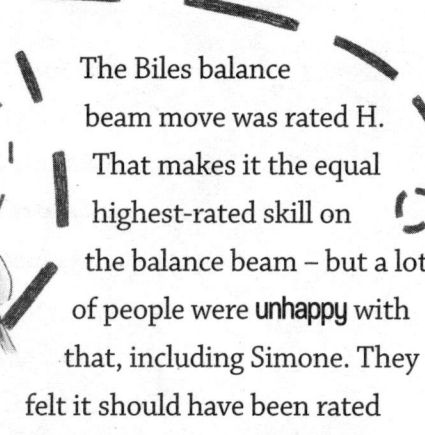

The Biles balance beam move was rated H. That makes it the equal highest-rated skill on the balance beam – but a lot of people were **unhappy** with that, including Simone. They felt it should have been rated even higher. The committee that did the scoring argued that they didn't want to give it too many points because they didn't want other people to try it! It was just too **dangerous** and **demanding** a move.

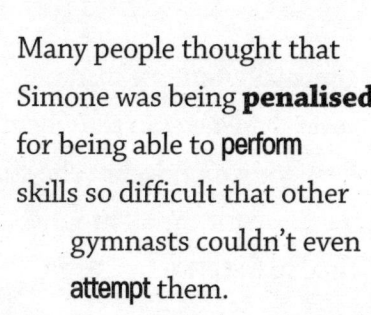

PLEASE don't try it!

Many people thought that Simone was being **penalised** for being able to **perform** skills so difficult that other gymnasts couldn't even **attempt** them.

She won five gold medals at that World Championships, making her the most **decorated** female gymnast in history.

The COVID-19 pandemic meant the 2020 Tokyo Olympics was postponed to 2021. Before the Olympics, Simone set another record in the US Classic competition by being the first woman to complete a Yurchenko double pike vault.

It was rated 6.6, the most difficult vault in women's gymnastics. Now she just needed to perform it at Tokyo to have it named the Biles II.

Unusually, Simone made several mistakes in the Olympics qualifying rounds, but she still qualified for the all-around final in first place.

She wasn't feeling good, though. She wrote on social media that she was struggling under the **pressure**. Then, in the team final, she made a mistake in the vault and almost fell. She withdrew from the team final, saying she had mental health issues. Then she went on to withdraw from nearly **all** her individual events too.

What had gone **wrong**?

Simone was under huge pressure and suffering from anxiety. She'd recently lost her beloved aunt. And, she revealed, she had another **problem**: 'the twisties'.

The 'twisties'

The 'twisties' is the name gymnasts have for a strange problem that makes them lose their sense of space in mid-air. Imagine you're flying through the air, flipping over and around at the same time in a complicated movement – but suddenly you don't know where you are. You might do more twists than you should, or forget a flip. You might not be able to land safely because your body is in the wrong place.

Hmm ... my air sense!

Uh oh!

In the Biles floor move, the gymnast does a half twist that means she can't see where she lands. Simone's coach said she could do that safely because she had good 'air sense'. But the twisties took that air sense away.

ARGH! Twisties!

It can be incredibly dangerous. US gymnast Jacoby Miles attempted a **difficult movement** while struggling with the twisties. She landed badly and broke her neck, leaving her **paralysed**.

Don't do it unless you feel safe!

JACOBY MILES

Gymnasts all agreed that Simone did the right thing by withdrawing from events. But a lot of people who wanted the US to win lots of medals were very **angry**. Journalists and politicians **criticised** her and told her that she should keep going, no matter what. Many people wrote horrible things about her on social media and called her a quitter. The global pressure to carry on was huge, and many people would have bowed to it. Refusing to perform was probably one of the **bravest acts** of Simone's life. She **stood up**, not only for herself, but for all athletes who need to take **care** of themselves.

And she didn't **give up**, despite having the twisties. She insisted on performing in the beam final, because those movements didn't require so much flipping and turning. She had to adjust her routine to make it **easier** than her usual one, and she still took a bronze medal. That meant she tied with Soviet gymnast Larisa Latynina for the most medals **ever** won by a female gymnast.

For Simone, that single bronze medal meant more to her than all her gold medals because it represented her **focus** on mental health and her **perseverance**.

She took a formal **break** from gymnastics after Tokyo, focusing on her mental health and on spending time with her family and friends. She **deserved** it!

Simone Biles has an incredible **haul** of gold medals and titles, and has had movements named after her at the **highest** level of difficulty.

She is a **world-class athlete** who has **overcome** many difficult experiences and dealt with mental health conditions to reach the top and stay there for years.

And she is a woman who had the courage to look the world in the face, under unimaginable pressure, and say, 'I will look after myself. I will do what is **right** for **me**.'

All our fantastically great women sports stars **achieved** amazing things for themselves. But each of them also changed the world for other people. They shared their winnings, their knowledge and their skills. They fought for women in sport, and **inspired** girls to start playing. They helped change other people's ideas of what's possible.

"It means more than all of the golds because I pushed through so much the last five years and the last week while I've even been here."

173

BE INSPIRED!

EXHIBITION OF EXCEP

Don't be afraid to take the plunge!

ELLIE SIMMONDS

Aim for new heights!

JUNKO TABEI

Whatever you do, give it your all!

CHARLOTTE 'LOTTIE' DODD

Don't let anyone tell you that you can't!

CYNISCA

174

You CAN go the distance!

DERARTU TULU

We're STRONGER together!

ALICE MILLIAT

Trust in yourself and you will go far!

MARTA VIEIRA DA SILVA

Be bold! Be brave! Be yourself!

SIMONE BILES

Other FANTASTICALLY GREAT ATHLETES...

This book includes just a few fantastically great women sports stars, but there are loads more! From surfers and skateboarders to cyclists and tennis-stars, women have been winning in sports and continue to do so all around the world. Could you be next?

Here are just a few more women to inspire you!

Bethany Hamilton – American professional surfer who returned to competing just two and a half months after a shark bit her arm off!

Jaiyah Saelua – American Samoan footballer. Jaiyah identifies as fa'afafine (a third gender in Samoan culture) and is the first trans woman to play in a FIFA World Cup qualifier. The story of how she and her teammates brought glory to the American Samoan team has been made into two films!

Karnam Malleswari – Two-time weightlifting world champion and the first Indian woman (and first Indian weightlifter) to win an Olympic medal.

176

Mayumi Narita – Japanese Paralympian swimmer who has won 15 Paralympic gold medals and was awarded Best Female Athlete by the International Paralympic Committee in 2005.

Sky Brown – British-Japanese professional skateboarder and Britain's youngest ever Olympic medallist!

Venus and Serena Williams – World-beating tennis players, who have both been ranked world no.1 in singles and doubles. Venus has won seven Grand Slam singles titles. Serena has won 23. Together, they have won 14 doubles Grand Slams, and they each hold four Olympic gold medals!

Wilma Rudolph – American sprinter who won three gold medals at Rome Olympics, 1960. As the fastest woman in the world, she was a role model for Black Americans, and campaigned for civil rights and women's rights.

Yusra Mardini – Former professional swimmer and refugee of the Syrian civil war, she competed in Tokyo 2020 with the Refugee Olympic Team. This team was made up of people from all over the world who have been forced to flee their home countries due to war, violence or political issues.

GLOSSARY

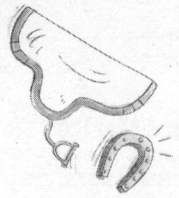

Acrobatics – the art of performing difficult feats of gymnastics. See also **Gymnastics**

Adopt – When a person or couple becomes a parent to a child who can no loner live with their birth parents

Agent – person who manages business or financial matters for a sports player

Altitude – the height of something above sea level

Ancient Olympic Games – a series of athletics competitions in ancient Greece, which took place every four years between 776 BCE and 393 CE

Anxiety – feelings of nervousness or fear which are hard to control

Apartheid – a policy of racial inequality in South Africa between 1948 and the early 1990s

Archer – a person who shoots with bows and arrows, usually in sports competitions

Ascent – climbing to the top of a hill or mountain

Athletics – a group of sporting competitions including running, jumping, throwing and walking

Boycott – when someone refuses to buy or take part in something as an act of protest

Coach – someone who trains another person in a sport

Contract – a legal agreement describing certain requirements between two or more people/groups

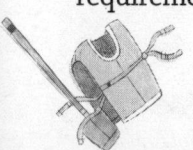

Decorated (awards) – when someone has a lot of medals or honours for doing something

Discus throw – a sport where competitors try to throw a heavy metal disc as far as possible

Federation – a group of organisations which have joined together to create a bigger organisation

FIFA – the organisation which governs international football teams and organises the World Cup

Flagbearer – person who carries the flag of their country during an important ceremony (e.g. Olympic Games)

Foster care – a system which places children in temporary homes when their parents have died or are unable to look after them

Freeborn – someone who wasn't born into slavery

Freestyle event – a sporting event where the competitor can choose what style or method they use

Gymnastics – a sport where performers do exercises – like flips, spins and jumps in the air or on special equipment – to display strength, balance and agility

Hippodrome – an oval arena with a track for horse races and chariot events

Individual medley – a swimming race where competitors swim each part of the course with a different stroke

Javelin – a light, pointy spear thrown in sports contests

Language barrier – when someone struggles to understand information because it is in a language they do not know or speak

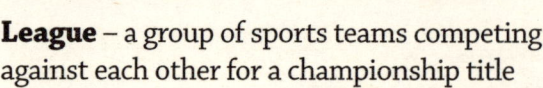

League – a group of sports teams competing against each other for a championship title

Loophole – a mistake or unclear phrase in a law or set of rules, which someone uses to get around the rule or law

Marathon – a long-distance running race of 26 miles

Member of the Order of the British Empire (MBE) – an honour from the British king or queen for outstanding achievement or service to the community

Mental health – a person's emotional and behavioural well-being

Modern Olympic Games – the largest international, multi-sport event in the world, takes place every four years

Myth – a traditional story, usually about supernatural or legendary people or creatures

Order of the British Empire (OBE) – an honour from the British king or queen for outstanding contributions to science and art or charitable work

Paralympic Games – the largest international, multi-sport event in the world for athletes with disabilities

Paralysed – when someone's body is partly or completely incapable of moving

Patron – someone who gives support to a person, group or organisation, usually by giving them money

Penalty – a disadvantage that a team or player is given for violating a rule – e.g. losing points

Pentathlon – an athletics competition which requires participants to compete in five separate contests

Poverty – when a person or group of people are extremely poor, and struggle to afford things like food or housing

Prejudice – a negative and unfair opinion of someone based on the group they belong to (like their race, gender, religion etc.)

Retire – when someone decides to stop working and leaves their job, normally when they reach a certain age or physical ability

Sacred – something considered to be holy and treated with great respect

Sea level – the average height of the sea's surface, which is used to calculate how high an area of land is

Spartan – people who lived in the ancient Greek city-state of Sparta

Sponsor /sponsorship – a person or company who provides funds for sports teams or events in exchange for the opportunity to advertise their business

Sports psychologist – a person who helps athletes achieve a high level of performance by supporting their mental health

Tournament – a competition with a series of games between teams or single competitors

Transfer (football) – when a professional football player moves from one football club to another

Translator – a person whose job is to change words from one language to another language

Try-outs – tests held by a coach to see if someone is skilled enough to join their sports team

FURTHER READING

If you want to find out more about any of the fantastically great women in this book, the books and websites below are brilliant resources.

BOOKS

Browne, Charlotte. (2019), *Marta (Ultimate Football Heroes)*. Dino Books.

Ignotofsky, Rachel. (2018), *Women in Sport: Fifty Fearless Athletes Who Played to Win*. Wren & Rook.

Pankhurst, Kate. (2016), *Fantastically Great Women Who Changed the World*. London: Bloomsbury.

Pankhurst, Kate. (2018), *Fantastically Great Women Who Made History*. London: Bloomsbury.

Pankhurst, Kate. (2019), *Fantastically Great Women Who Worked Wonders*. London: Bloomsbury.

Pankhurst, Kate (2020), *Fantastically Great Women Who Saved the Planet*. Bloomsbury.

Nuñez, Jhonny (2021), *The Ancient Olympic Games*. Wayland.

Rebel Girls (2020), *Junko Tabei Masters the Mountains*. Rebel Girls.

Rebel Girls (2021), ***Rebel Girls Champion: 25 Tales of Unstoppable Athletes.*** Rebel Girls.

Sanchez Vegara, Maria Isabel (2024), ***Simone Biles (Little People BIG DREAMS)***. Francis Lincoln.

Woodfine, Katherine and Okstad, Ella. (2024), ***Lottie the Little Wonder: the inspiring story of tennis superstar Lottie Dod*** (Little Gems). Barrington Stoke.

WEBSITES

BBC Bitesize. https://www.bbc.co.uk/bitesize

Britannica Kids. https://kids.britannica.com

Olympic Games. https://olympics.com/

Paralympic Games. https://www.paralympic.org/

UN Women. https://www.unwomen.org/en/news/in-focus/women-and-sport

Women in Football. https://www.womeninfootball.co.uk/

Thank yous!

This book has been a long time in the planning and creating but I'm SO delighted that we now have a Fantastically Great Women book focusing on sport. It feels like we are living in a golden moment for women's sport – and in a golden opportunity to INSPIRE the children who will be the next generation of Olympians, footballers, athletes and more.

As I watched the England women's football team, the Lionesses, win the Women's Euros in 2022 and smash their way to the final of the Women's World Cup in 2023, I thought of how different things were when I was younger and how amazing it is that children today have so many opportunities to watch incredible women at the absolute top of the game.

I wanted to dedicate this book to the children at my local football club – Calverley United Juniors girls' and boys' teams. It has been an absolute joy to see so many local girls finding a love for football, growing in confidence (on and off the pitch) and supporting each other across both boys and girls teams. The coaches and volunteers running the club are doing so much to encourage a life-long love of sport and to bring more girls into the game.

There are so many people I'd like to thank for their role in getting this book off the starting blocks to the finish line. A Fantastically Great trophy to the amazing duo of my editor Emily Ball and my designer Katie Knutton at Bloomsbury for getting this book into shape. Our weekly catch-ups, juggling of deadlines and endless ideas have been such a massive help in making this book happen.

Medals all round to rest of the editorial team at Bloomsbury who have done so much to support the vast amount of research involved in this book and to the marketing and publicity team for finding ever inventive ways to make sure everybody knows it now exists.

A huge thank you, round of applause and special laurel wreath for Kate Paice and Damien Barlow for their energy, commitment and creative contributions to this book.

And lastly, there wouldn't be a Fantastically Great Women series without my incredible agents at Plum Illustration Agency. I am endlessly grateful we had a chat about my Pankhurst connections back in 2015. A big thank you to Hannah Whitty, Mark Mills and the whole Plum team. It's been a journey and it's not over yet!

Kate Pankhurst, March 2024

Also in this series ...

From the BESTSELLING author

Kate Pankhurst

FANTASTICALLY

GREAT WOMEN SCIENTISTS

and their STORIES

BLOOMSBURY

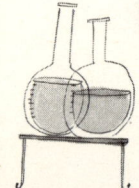

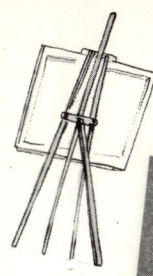

From the BESTSELLING author

Kate Pankhurst

FANTASTICALLY

GREAT
WOMEN
ARTISTS

and their
STORIES

BLOOMSBURY

Fantastically
Great Women
Who Changed
the World

Fantastically
Great Women
Who Made
History

Fantastically
Great Women
Who Worked
Wonders

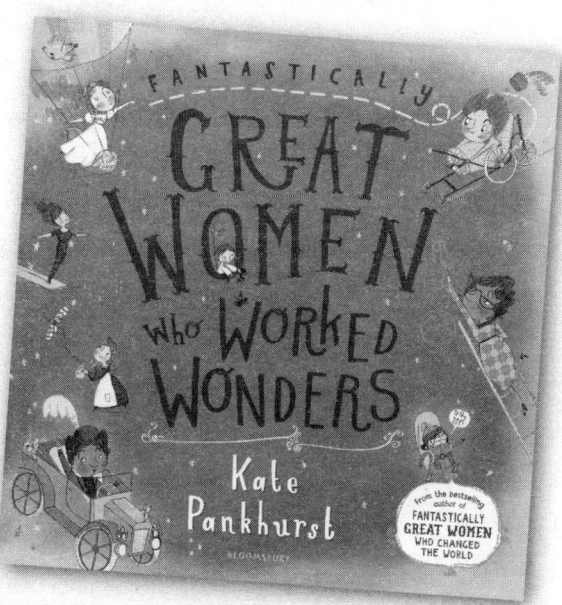

Fantastically
Great Women
Who Saved
the Planet

In Kate Pankhurst's

WE ARE ALL

Series

WE ARE ALL ASTRONAUTS!

Discover what it takes to be a space explorer!

KATE PANKHURST

THE BESTSELLING author of

FANTASTICALLY GREAT WOMEN

BLOOMSBURY

We Are All Astronauts!

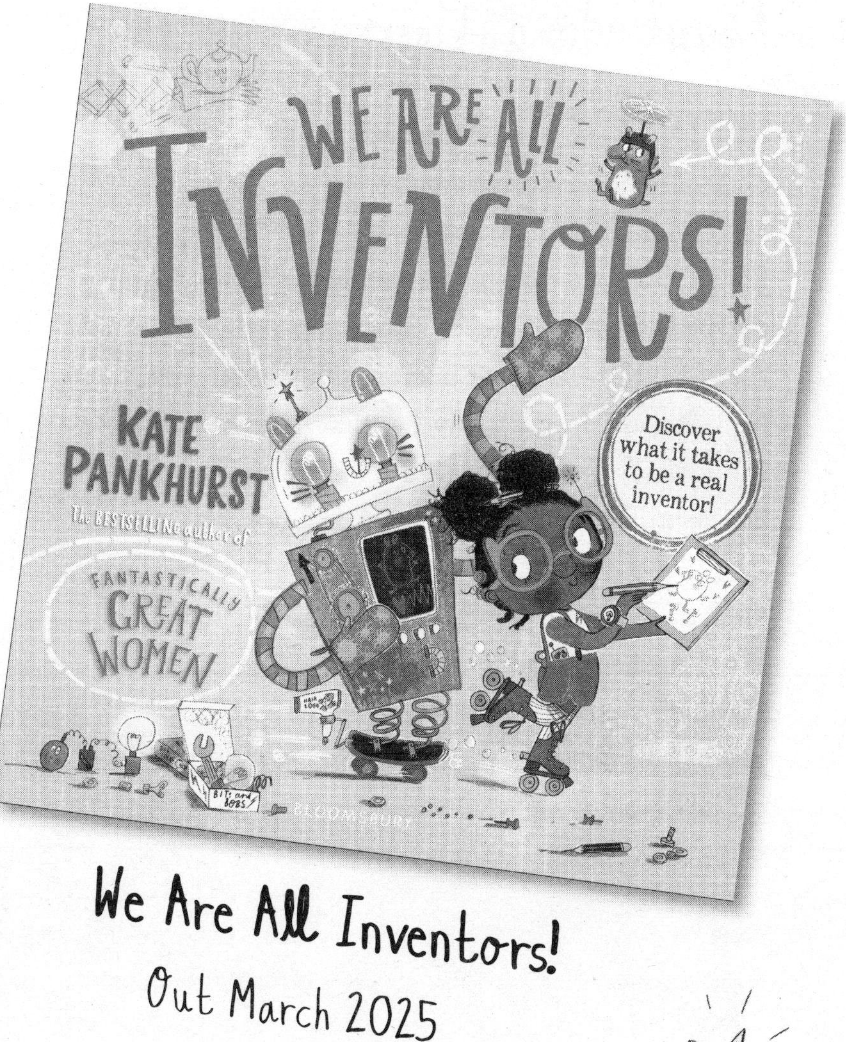

We Are All Inventors!
Out March 2025

About the author

KATE PANKHURST is the bestselling author and illustrator of the trailblazing and internationally successful **FANTASTICALLY GREAT WOMEN** books. Kate's books have been translated into 22 languages and been shortlisted for many awards, including the NIBBIES award for Children's Illustrated and Non-fiction. Most recently, her first book, *Fantastically Great Women who Changed the World*, has been adapted into an inspiring stage show.

Most days, Kate can be found illustrating and writing in her studio in Leeds with her spotty dog, Olive. She loves a good story, the funnier the better, and gets her best ideas by doodling in her sketchbook; because even quick, wonky drawings can spark ideas for amazing plots.